Dr David Cotton

Climate Change
a wake up call

GW00701602

An environmentally friendly book printed and bound in England by
www.printondemand-worldwide.com

Mixed Sources
Product group from well-managed
forests, and other controlled sources
www.fsc.org Cert no. TT-COC-002641
© 1996 Forest Stewardship Council

FSC

PEFC
PEFC/16-33-415

PEFC Certified

This product is
from sustainably
managed forests
and controlled
sources

www.pefc.org

This book is made entirely of chain-of-custody materials

www.fast-print.net/store.php

CLIMATE CHANGE: A WAKE-UP CALL
Copyright © David Cotton 2015

A catalogue record for this book is available from the British Library

ISBN 978-178456-163-5

First published 2015 by
Fastprint Publishing of Peterborough, England.

This book is dedicated to my two sons, Patrick and Dominic, and to my four grandsons, Sam, Finn, Jack and Oscar. The planet's future continues to be far more important for them than it will be for me.

Contents

The Author - Dr David Cotton

David Cotton, born in 1940 and educated at King's School, Worcester and Worcester College, Oxford. He left Oxford with an MA in Chemistry and a DPhil for research into the thermal decomposition of hydrocarbons.

He continued in Research for three years with Shell looking into the formation of smoke in flames, diesel engines and gas turbines and how it could be prevented. This work led to the publication of papers in scientific journals including The Proceedings of the Royal Society, Transactions of the Faraday Society, Science Progress and Nature

He moved into more commercial activities with Shell International and was part of a team responsible for thinking up new products the company might make.

David joined Metra Martech in 1975 and has worked with them since then as a business and marketing consultant. Almost all this work has been concerned with technical products in areas as varied as pharmaceuticals, computers and alternative fuels.

Work at Metra led to increasing involvement in data analysis, interpretation and forecasting as well as in the presentation of results. Using these skills to analyse information on the climate he wrote "Climate Change - what you need to know". This detailed look at the global situation and likely developments over the next 100 years was published in 2010. The present volume is a condensed and updated version of the earlier book. It concentrates on the consequences of Global Warming, on ways of slowing it down and the opportunities which exist to manage the problems.

David remains concerned about the issue of Global Warming and the adequate availability of energy. We **MUST** wake up now and we **MUST** take serious steps to rapidly reduce our consumption of fossil fuels. We **MUST** greatly accelerate the rate at which we are developing sources of renewable energy. David believes that the problem can be managed in the future if we really try and if we are prepared to cooperate internationally. However, he is very concerned that not all the major players will come on board in time to take the necessary steps quickly enough.

Acknowledgements

Firstly I must acknowledge three exceptional teachers at school who each, in their own eccentric ways, inspired me with the curiosity without which I would not have studied science.

My earlier publication took four years to put together, and the present volume would not have evolved without the support I had in writing the first one. This volume has taken a further four year to complete and has involved considerable updating of data and refinement of the conclusions. In particular, I must thank my wife, Gail, for her encouragement. She has read through many drafts making valuable suggestions about better presentation of ideas. Her brother, Alan Thompson, a lecturer in languages at the Tampere University of Technology in Finland has put me right on many points of grammar and presentation. My old friend, Michael Rock, has always been there to advise on presentation of particular concepts. Another friend, Nick van der Borgh, a lawyer, has been invaluable as an "intelligent layman". He has helped me to appreciate the level of detail that is appropriate and what will be interesting and comprehensible to someone who, like himself, does not have specific scientific knowledge.

Despite all this support, any shortcomings or errors remain entirely my own responsibility.

Preface

"The Will of the People" is something our democratically elected politicians are continually urged to take into account, whether the issue is the introduction of identity cards or confronting Global Warming. When people are offered organic food or are considering medical advice, they are told they should make an "informed choice" but such decisions are frequently clouded by political preference or expediency. The best solutions are often confused by hype and hysteria. So how do ordinary people become "informed" on subjects that experts have spent their lives exploring? First and foremost, we need some understanding of the background to the questions, whatever they may be.

Many important questions facing the World today are economic, cultural or political in nature, but there are others where a scientific background is needed to appreciate the options. Science is as prone to disagreement and controversy as any other topic and it is an area about which members of the general public are often woefully ignorant.

Climate Change is caused, in part, by greenhouse gases but what are they and how do they work? We are sometimes told that hydrogen fuelled cars will reduce Global Warming, but will they and, if so, why? Since man first walked the planet around 500,000 years ago, the World population had reached three billion by 1960. Since then it has more than doubled to over seven billion. Can there be an end to the population explosion? When oil runs out, as in the end it must, what are the alternative fuels? Will there be enough of them and is there an environmental downside to their use? Are there other resources which are in short supply?

It is important for us to understand the issues and to encourage politicians and decision makers to take appropriate actions and it is also important to support them when necessary. It is also important that the next generation of voters understand the issues. This book is aimed at both inquiring adults and the youth who will step into our shoes in a few years time.

This book is concerned with three crucial issues:
- Is the climate changing and if so how fast?
- How much energy will the World population need in the future?
- How can we provide all the energy which will be needed without seriously disrupting the climate?

To reach realistic conclusions on these questions some understanding of science and statistics is needed. My object in writing this book is to provide enough background for people to appreciate the issues and uncertainties involved. Armed with this information they will be better able to reach a reasoned opinion and to recognise when realistic policies are being proposed - it is crucial that the policies adopted are both achievable and effective. The Kyoto Protocol, an international agreement which has evolved since the 1990s is a step towards controlling greenhouse gases. The targets agreed may be achievable but there are few scientists now who believe they are strict enough to have more than a very minor impact on Global Warming. Only a handful of countries have taken concrete steps even to meet these very modest targets.

Limiting the Global temperature rise to an acceptable level will involve all governments adopting policies which although they have long term benefits they also have short term costs. This will be difficult but the more people understand the problems the easier it will be. Of course, environmental issues are not the only serious questions, scientific or otherwise, that are facing the World today but they are very important. If more people understand the principles, there is a greater probability of our adopting effective policies and accepting their consequences. Widespread international cooperation is vital for the resolution of these questions.

I began research for my first book eight years ago and at that time I was unsure whether man had a significant role in causing Global Warming. As my research has continued, I have become more and more convinced that our activities are making a significant contribution to the problem. However, I also believe that there are opportunities for solving the problems and ultimate disaster is not inevitable. But we are not developing renewable energy sources nearly fast enough and there is an urgent need for Global action to begin now – **hence this wake up call.** Will all the major players come on board quickly enough to avoid serious consequences?

I have not set out to convince you dogmatically of my own opinions. I have presented the evidence so that you will be able to reach your own conclusions and I trust that these will, in the end, be the same as mine!

DHC London – March 2015

vi

Chapter 1

Introduction

Setting The Scene

At some distant point in time, life on Earth will come to end. The Sun will eventually burn itself out or the universe will collapse back into the black hole from which it originated. In the meantime, some people argue, Global Warming has the potential to change the climate so much that Mankind is wiped out in the next few hundred years. It could be argued that since life will, at some point come to an end, it makes no real difference when that happens - the final result is just the same. However, most of us would probably agree that it's a "good thing" for the Human Race to continue its existence for as long as possible into the future.

Most educated people have the knowledge to debate political or economic questions with some degree of understanding and to reach their own "informed" opinion. The range of opinions even among well informed people is, however, usually large and there is seldom one "right" answer to any particular question. Other issues often require some specialist knowledge to arrive at an "informed" opinion and Global Warming and Climate Change are examples of issues where some specific knowledge is essential. They are also issues where global cooperation is of paramount importance if suitable mitigating policies are to be agreed and implemented. A single country can, within limits, raise the living standards of its people or eliminate poverty without being dependent on other countries. A single country, however, cannot significantly affect its climate without the cooperation of most of the other nations in the World.

Coverage in the media of the issues of Global Warming and Climate Change has increased in recent years although it is often spasmodic and frequently overshadowed by the economic problems which have arisen in the last six years. Unfortunately, short-term issues almost always take precedence over the long-term ones even when the latter are ultimately of much greater importance. However, one newspaper in the UK identified

1

the Climate Change conference due in Paris next autumn as one of the key events of 2015 and the Pope has been recognising the urgent need for Climate Action. I am not alone in making a "Wake Up Call"

There are still "sceptics" who deny that there is any significant change in climate or that Mankind has anything to with it. There are also "catastrophists" who claim that whatever we do now, disaster will strike many parts of the World within a decade. In between is a broad band of opinion, which accepts that Mankind is disturbing the climate, largely as a consequence of burning fossil fuels and the release of greenhouse gases (GHGs). It is also widely accepted that we can and should do something about it. However, there is considerable reluctance to agree to any steps which cause short-term inconvenience or which cost money now even if, in the long-term, they will lead to savings. Getting politicians to make the crucial decisions is a major difficulty as discussed in Chapter 12.

The level of acceptance varies from country to country. In the USA concern is often expressed that controlling Climate Change would adversely affect their economy and so governments are reluctant to commit themselves to the steps needed but recently some major US politicians have begun to recognise that action is needed. In emerging economies, there is a reluctance to do anything about it while we, in the Developed World, continue our profligate consumption of fossils fuels. There are some moves to get the rich countries to fund necessary developments in poor countries. There are definite signs that attitudes are changing in, for example, China but how adequate are the targets.

Some people see it as their "right" to use as much energy as they want so long as they can pay for it while others think we have left it too late to do anything useful. On a recent Climate Change demonstration I heard a fellow marcher in a heated debate with a bystander who took the view that it is already too late and that anything we do will be instantly offset by the Chinese opening yet another coalmine. Our only choice was, he said, to enjoy ourselves while we can and hard luck on future generations.

Global Cooperation

As already remarked, the key point to recognise is that we must make a concerted effort, at a global level, to have any significant impact on the climate. International cooperation is vital. To achieve this we will have to abandon some of our more selfish attitudes both at personal and national levels. As I argue in some detail in Chapter 12, we have to drop our continuing struggle for economic growth in the Developed World, and accept that more is not necessarily better.

Substantial change has to be led by governments, but if enough of us show concern for the issue, then politicians will adopt appropriate policies to attract our votes. To what extent are governments prepared to put the long-term good of the planet ahead of short-term political gain? Politicians in many countries are beginning to announce initiatives they plan to adopt to address environmental issues. However, we have to ensure that these policies are being effectively implemented and that our leaders are not merely paying lip service to global welfare in order to attract more votes. Of course, it is up to us the voters, to elect governments who take the global view - then the two aims will coincide.

Achieving international cooperation is an order of magnitude more difficult than influencing national policies but it has to be done. The Kyoto Protocol, drawn up in Japan in 1997, was an attempt to set some targets for lowering our emission of greenhouse gases (GHGs) by 2012. Many would argue that the targets were much too modest but there have been further conferences which set out to update the Kyoto targets. These conferences in Copenhagen (2009), Cancun (2010) and Durban (2011) failed to reach agreement and merely postponed to 2015 the date when the targets would be updated. The Doha (2012) conference confirmed this postponement while at the Warsaw (2013) conference it was agreed that the Lima (2014) conference would draft targets to be finalised at the 2015 conference to be held in Paris. Lima concluded with a "Call for Climate Action" which now has to be finalised in Paris. In addition there was the UN Climate Change Summit in 2014 which made some encouraging noises. The right noises are being made but we are still waiting for much more concrete action.

There are strong economic pressures to maintain the status quo but the Stern Review, published in the UK, considers that such arguments are only valid in the short-term. If we take a longer-term view then there are real economic arguments for taking steps now to control Global Warming. The UN Climate Change Summit held in September 2014 had interesting ideas and began the process for agreeing a Global Climate Change strategy in Paris in 2015. What can we do to ensure that the steps agreed will be taken seriously and that they will be implemented?

Again I stress that serious global cooperation will be essential to limit Climate Change and those of us who are better off will also have to accept that economic growth will not go on forever. Indeed, we may even need to share some of our wealth with those who have so much less. How many of us in the Developed World are prepared to accept this?

The Three Questions

There are some dangers, such as earthquakes and volcanoes, over which we have no control but there are other dangers we can manage. Initially there were very gloomy forecasts about the likely consequences of pandemics such as Avian flu, SARS or HIV/AIDS. Of course, they have had their victims but, in global terms, they have been kept under control, largely as a result of international cooperation. It remains to be seen how the Ebola virus will develop. Global Warming is another risk which the World has to face. The consequences can be controlled but only if we get worldwide agreement on what needs to be done and then we do it. The pandemics referred to above have immediate consequences so we get immediate global action. The consequences of Global Warming are less immediately dramatic so we can all go on delaying our response.

The climate, whether changing or not, is a very complex matter. To arrive at an "informed" opinion on Climate Change, rather than just a prejudice, we need some appreciation of the basic scientific ideas. My aim in writing this book is to present some background to help you reach such an opinion for yourself. You will not become an expert (unless you read a lot of other books) but you may begin to see when the wool is being pulled over your eyes or when a protagonist has a particular, often economic, axe to grind.

One of the things I often find lacking in discussions of Global Warming is a quantitative look at what the impact of particular actions will be in terms of both the energy saved and the effect on our lifestyle. This applies at an individual, a national and, particularly, at a global level. All the main political parties in the UK have recently suggested that we will have to cut our release of carbon dioxide (CO_2) into the atmosphere by 20% by 2030 and by 80% by 2050. The figures are similar to those suggested by the

UK Committee on Climate Change. The Green Party is suggesting we need to make a cut of 95% by 2050. What we need is some indication of what these reductions would mean in practical terms, what it would cost and what we might be able to use as alternative sources of energy.

In summary, this book addresses three questions:

- **Is Global Warming a reality and will it have a serious adverse impact on Mankind** - how fast is it happening and why? What will this do to the climate and is Mankind responsible?
- **How much energy will the World need** - as a result of increases in both population and in individual consumption? How will this impact on the use of fossils fuels and hence on Global Warming?
- **Where will our energy come from** - what sources can we use instead of fossil fuels to meet our needs while at the same time limiting Global Warming? How do we develop these alternatives and how quickly will we need them?

The debate is under way but without some understanding of the principles, we may end up with uninformed and misleading conclusions and we may adopt counter-productive policies. We have to recognise that there are at least two sides to most arguments and we have to be prepared to adjust our own ideas and conclusions as new information comes to light.

There are a number of references to classification of countries in different groups, Developed, Developing, G8, G20 etc. The countries in each group are listed in Appendix A. A variety of acronyms are used throughout the text. Regularly used ones are defined in Appendix B

An Overview

There is some deliberate repetition so that each chapter can be read alone without you necessarily having to read all the previous chapters.

Chapter 2 looks at why we have a climate and the factors which interact to give us such wide global and seasonal variations. In particular, I have explained the role of GHGs and how they are related to fossil fuels.

Chapter 3 is an historical look at climate data and the evidence for the impact of Human activities. It covers trends in global temperature over half a million years as well as the much more recent pattern.

Chapter 4 considers where fossil fuels have come from and how their use has developed over the last 200 years. This chapter illustrates the dramatic rate at which production and consumption of these fuels has increased. It includes sections on where the known reserves are and how long they will last. It also considers the political tensions which may arise as resources become exhausted.

Chapter 5 looks at different types of energy and how, in principle, each type can be used. I have also considered practical and theoretical efficiencies as well as the impact of different fossils fuels on the build up of CO_2 in the atmosphere.

Chapter 6 begins with an overall look at the global carbon footprint and how it varies from region to region. Most of the chapter, however, is a detailed look at the carbon footprint in the UK for which extensive data is available. What are the main components and what are the steps that can be taken to reduce both individual and national footprints?

Chapter 7 is concerned with population. The World population has more than doubled since 1960 and the term "Population Explosion" is not an exaggeration. This chapter looks at the past as a clue to where population may be going and uses UNDP forecasts which suggest there is a chance that global population may stabilise at around 10 billion before 2100. Some recent projections suggest that this may be unduly optimistic and it may reach 15 billion. How will this affect the climate?

Chapter 8 presents forecasts of Global Warming I have developed, based on various assumptions about energy demand and fossil fuel consumption in the future and how this may affect the climate in the long-term. It is at this point that it becomes apparent that a serious problem is developing.

Chapter 9 looks at the energy we will need in the future taking into account growth in population and the increase in per capita consumption as the poorer parts of the world catch up with the Developed Countries. I have estimated how demand for renewables will need to develop to keep the future temperature rise to less than 1°C or 2°C above the present level.

Chapter 10 looks at the potential sources of renewable energy and describes, in outline, how each one works. I have looked at some of the downsides of each as well as giving an estimate of the amount of energy we might be able to harvest in the future. I have also considered how the energy can be delivered when and where it is needed. Even if the population doubles again there could still be enough renewable energy around if only we can develop effective ways of harvesting it. There is a solution to the problem but only if we choose to solve it.

Chapter 11 looks at the attempts we have made so far to reduce the use of fossil fuels and to encourage development of renewables. The Kyoto Protocol has achieved little to date and subsequent conferences have so far added nothing concrete. This chapter emphasises the need for global cooperation and the need for very rapid action now to develop renewables.

In **Chapter 12** I have considered the key principles that must be built into any plan for the future including the more equitable distribution of energy and wealth between regions and limiting the eternal quest, in Developed Countries, for economic growth. I have also considered how conflict of interest, both nationally and internationally, might be dealt with and the possible process by which a global plan might be agreed. This is not, of course, a definitive solution but only a suggested starting point.

A Wake Up Call

Mankind can have a direct influence on Climate Change and when we understand the underlying principles, we are much better able to understand the implications of different policies and lobby our leaders to take action. Although we may be able to see what needs to be done, it will still require political will and a concerted effort by every nation to arrive at a successful outcome.

The discussion in this book focuses on the worldwide picture so as to identify global needs and solutions. When it comes to implementing solutions each country will have to develop policies which meet their local needs while still taking into account what is required internationally.

My final conclusion is that there are feasible ways of supplying the energy we need to maintain an acceptable and more equitable standard of living around the World. My major concern is that we will not move quickly enough and we will not cooperate sufficiently to avoid the potential disaster which could arise in the next fifty years. Am I naive in thinking that the level of international cooperation required is even a possibility.

This is a **WAKE UP CALL**. We have to take serious action and we have to begin now.

Chapter 2

Why We Have A Climate

A Delicate Balance

Our climate is largely determined by the heat from the sun which gives rise to complex and competing forces in a thin layer of the atmosphere over the Earth's surface known as the Troposphere. This layer, is less than 20 km thick and has the same relative thickness as a layer of eggshell over a football! The oceans depths also contribute to the climate.

We know that it's hotter at the equator than at the poles but the extremes are not always at these places. The highest surface temperature ever recorded is 57.8°C at Azizia in Libya, 1,000 km north of the equator. The lowest temperature is -90°C at Vostok, 1,300 km from the South Pole. Florida on the same latitude as the Sahara has a very different climate while London, as far north as Labrador, is, thankfully, very much warmer than the latter.

The "Weather" at a given moment is defined by the temperature, humidity, wind speed and direction, cloud cover and sunshine and whether or not it is raining or snowing etc. The weather changes with the seasons and, within the cycle, there are daily variations. The climate, in a given area, is the sum of the weather over the years and there is no simple way of describing it in one place let alone over the whole World. How then can we measure whether there really is any Climate Change?

The Earth's Temperature

The Earth's temperature depends on the balance of energy between the Sun, the Earth and the rest of space as illustrated on the next page. Imagine the Earth with no atmosphere. When solar energy, sunlight, hits the surface, some is reflected while the rest is absorbed by the surface which becomes a little warmer. The Earth, like any other object, then emits energy from the warm surface back into space at a rate dependant on its temperature. Over time the temperature will adjust itself until the amount of energy emitted is the same as that absorbed. When this equilibrium is reached the temperature remains constant. Under these conditions, but without an atmosphere, the temperature at the Earth's surface would be about -18°C, much the same as the average on the moon.

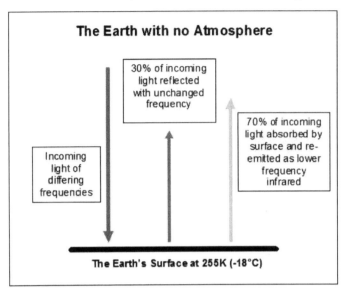

Fortunately, we do have an atmosphere which not only contains the oxygen essential for life, but which also acts as a blanket to keep us, on average, more than 30°C warmer than we would otherwise be. Crucially this means that there is liquid water in the oceans and rivers. The way the blanket operates is complex and although experts remain divided on some details many general facts are well established and agreed.

Radiation and Temperature

Any object radiates energy in the form of electromagnetic waves. This ranges from low frequency, infra-red radiation, through mid-frequency visible light to high frequency ultra violet. The amount of energy emitted is strongly dependant on the temperature. The hotter the object the greater the amount of energy released and the higher its frequency. At first when you heat an iron bar with a blow lamp you can feel the infra-red radiation emitted from it if you put your hand near the surface but you cannot see any radiation. As you heat it more it begins to glow red and then as the temperature, and with it the frequency, increases further it becomes white hot.

When radiation hits a surface some of it is reflected but the rest is absorbed by the object causing it to get warmer. As it gets hotter the amount of energy re-emitted increases until the amount being emitted equals the amount of incoming energy being absorbed and the temperature remains constant. This is a state of equilibrium.

The diagram below shows the main atmospheric influences on the flow of energy. Clouds reflect some of the incoming radiation which would cool the Earth but the clouds also prevent some escape of radiation from the surface hence keeping the atmosphere warmer. Ice caps reflect more energy than the average while forests absorb more. Changes in either can affect the average temperature.

Naturally occurring greenhouse gases (GHGs) include primarily water and CO_2 and these have a significant impact. They are **transparent to incoming higher frequency sunlight but they absorb lower frequency infrared radiation**. Some of the sunlight hitting the atmosphere is reflected straight back into space with unchanged frequency but some passes through the atmosphere and is absorbed by the surface and then re-emitted as lower frequency infrared radiation. **Crucially some of this infrared radiation is absorbed by the GHGs and trapped in the atmosphere** in the same way that the glass in a greenhouse traps energy. The energy trapped by the GHGs, together with the effect of clouds, makes the atmosphere 30°C warmer than it would otherwise be, hence making the Earth a habitable place. Any increase in the concentration of GHGs means more energy is trapped making both the atmosphere and the surface slightly warmer and, potentially, leading to Climate Change.

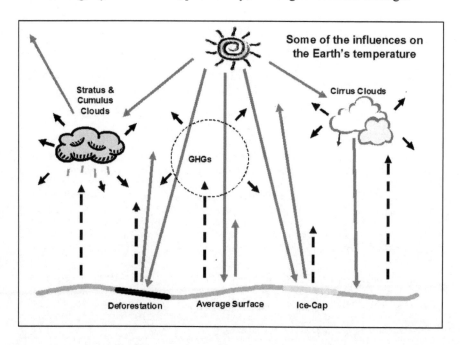

Atmospheric GHGs include water, CO_2, CH_4 (methane or natural gas), ozone and CFCs (chlorofluorocarbons). Water arises largely through evaporation from the oceans. CO_2 is dissolved in the sea as well as being in the air and there is an equilibrium between the two phases. Additional CO_2 comes from the burning of fossil fuels and from burning wood after deforestation. Ozone results from the interaction of oxides of nitrogen with other pollutants and CFCs come from leakage of refrigerants from old-fashioned cooling systems. CH_4 is produced when biological matter ferments and from both ends of cows and other ruminants as they digest their food. The most important man-made GHG is CO_2 and even a small increase in its concentration in the atmosphere can lead to small but significant changes in the atmospheric temperature.

Remember that GHGs overall keep the Earth 30°C warmer than it would otherwise be so an increase of only 3% in their overall concentration is likely to increase the temperature by one degree. It is important to realise that even a small increase in the level of GHGs is enough to have a significant impact on the global temperature.

Why The Wind Blows

In the discussion above the temperature of the atmosphere was talked about as if it were uniform across the whole globe. This is manifestly not true. The amount of heat imparted by the Sun depends on its angle in the sky. Over the year, a point on the equator receives three times as much energy as at either of the poles. The result, as we are well aware, is that

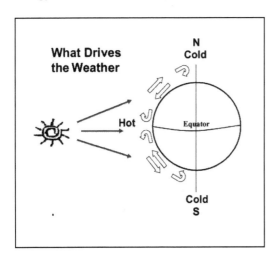

the Earth's surface, and the atmosphere above it, is much hotter in the tropics than at the poles. This difference is the primary driver for the weather.

As is well known hot air tends to rise by convection so there is an up-flow of air in the tropics creating a low-pressure zone which sucks in air from the poles with a corresponding down-flow of air over the poles. In principle, this will set up the convection currents as indicated in the diagram. Air flows over the surface from the poles to the tropics and then returns again at high altitude back to the poles. These currents go some way towards evening out the temperature differences between the equator and the poles.

In practice, it is not nearly as simple as this. Firstly the rotation of the Earth and with it the Coriolis effect, creates westerly winds at high altitude and easterly ones at the surface and the circulation between the equator and the poles splits into three separate cells. The surface of the Earth divides into three climate bands in both hemispheres each with either prevailing easterly or westerly winds. The location of these bands changes with the seasons. The distribution of land and sea and the height of mountains add further complications. The southern hemisphere, with only a quarter of the Earth's total land mass and with less interference from mountains has a very different climate from the northern hemisphere.

Ocean Currents

When heat is transferred between the sea and the atmosphere this affects the movement of the oceans and creates currents. The surface water is warmer at the equator than nearer the poles. Water expands as it gets warmer, so the surface is slightly higher (only 8 cm) at the equator than at mid latitudes. But this is enough to set up surface currents as the water runs away from the equator.

Wind blowing over the surface tends to take the water with it and the latter piles up against any land which obstructs the flow. When the wind eases or changes direction a current can be set up in the opposite direction as the water flows back the way it came.

The forces combine to set up relatively stable circulating systems (gyres), in the main ocean basins. One of these is the North Atlantic Gyre, known as the Gulf Stream, a spin off from which keep parts of North West Europe, including the UK, much warmer than they would otherwise be.

There are other gyres in the South Atlantic and the North and South Pacific, all of which have detailed characteristics determined by the local topography of the seabed and the air currents over their surface. These combine to impact on the global climate. Wind blowing eastwards across the Pacific builds up water against the West coast of South America. When the wind stops the water flows back creating cyclones in the atmosphere which can have a wide impact around the world. This particular effect is known as El Niño.

Where To Now?

The climate is a very complex matter and models to predict how it will change have to take into account GHGs, clouds and the reflectivity of the Earth's surface. They also have to include the impact of wind, currents and differences in terrain so it would be surprising if there were total agreement on the conclusions.

A model which takes all these factors into account and which is accurate enough to predict climate and weather as well as the impact of small increases in average temperature cannot be built from scratch. However, it is not necessary to rely on theory alone as observations and measurements that show what has happened in the past also allow extrapolations to be made into the future. Past changes and these extrapolations are covered in Chapter 3 and 8.

Chapter 3

Historical Climate Change

Mainstream scientific and political opinion now accepts that man-made Climate Change, or Anthropogenic Global Warming (AGW), is almost certainly a fact and that it began with the industrial revolution in the late seventeen hundreds. There are, however, still some sceptics who argue that AGW is not yet a proven fact.

To resolve the question we have to decide whether the climate has changed significantly in the last 200 years. If it has, can this be attributed to Human activities or is it just a continuation of changes which have been occurring naturally since the Earth began.

Measuring The Change – Temperature Anomalies

The climate is primarily influenced by latitude but it is also affected by the altitude, by the pattern of land across the planet, by local land usage and by proximity to the sea. The climate, of course, varies widely from place to place. The simplest parameter concerning the climate is the average temperature and if the annual average changes over the years this indicates a change in the climate. If we want to decide whether the global climate is changing then we need an average for the whole planet.

Today measurements are made using instruments operated under controlled conditions at specific locations and a continuous record can easily be kept, but instrumental measurements only go back to about 1860. There is little problem in calculating the average temperature at a specific location but converting this into a real global average is more difficult. We can only calculate a realistic average temperature if we have a large set of measurements from sites representative of the whole World - getting such a set going back through history is impossible.

The problem is overcome by calculating the "temperature anomaly" at a set of locations. The anomaly at a particular location is the difference between the current annual average temperature and the average over 30 years or more at some point in time. The average global anomaly, calculated from all the locations available, is an estimate of the average global temperature change. Note, this is not the same as calculating the average absolute temperature but it gives a meaningful indication of any change from a much smaller number of measurements than are necessary to calculate the real average.

Nowadays the temperature can be measured directly or it can be deduced from satellite measurements. To get temperatures before about 1860 we use proxy measurements which rely on measuring specific properties of some object and then using a logical scientific process to estimate the temperature when the object was created. The most common proxies for temperature are Tree Rings and Ice Cores but similar estimates can be made from coral reefs or boreholes through the Earth's surface or the seabed. These methods all give estimates of the temperature anomaly at a particular time and location. The significance of each set of measurements has to be considered individually so that we can arrive at a "best" answer for the global average.

Proxy Temperature Measurements

- Ice Cores

Ice cores can be used to estimate temperature anomalies back as far as 600,000 years. The most famous of these is at Vostok, 1,300 km from of the South Pole. Each year a fresh layer of snow falls. This never melts and is steadily compacted by subsequent layers. A core, more than 3,600 metres deep, has been extracted and by counting back through the layers the age of a particular layer can be established. The ratio of hydrogen to deuterium and the proportion of the heavy isotope of oxygen, ^{18}O, can be used to calculate the temperature at the time when that layer was formed.

Bubbles of air were trapped in the snow flakes as they fell. This air, from a set of adjacent layers, can be collected and analysed. The proportion of CO_2 in this sample is the same as that in the global atmosphere at the time the layer was formed. We thus have an historic measure of the change in both the atmospheric temperature and the level of CO_2 going back 600,000 years.

- Tree Rings

Each year a tree adds another layer of wood beneath its bark to form a new ring for each year. The thickness and density of a ring is very sensitive to the temperature during each growing period. The ring properties can be measured and a rolling average can be calculated for each year in the tree's life. From the temperature measured for recent years the scale can be calibrated and an estimate made of the temperature anomaly at the tree's location going back through history. Some trees live a very long time and the range can be extended back 1,000 years by matching the ring pattern in long dead trees to that in living trees where lifetimes overlap. Bristlecone pines are the longest living trees and by matching a sequence of dead trees, estimates of the temperature anomaly back 9,000 years have been made.

Long Term Changes

Throughout history there have been changes in the climate. There have been four major ice ages and we are currently in the fifth, which began about 40 million years ago. Within each ice age, there have been considerable temperature fluctuations with glacial and interglacial periods of varying severity.

Analysis of the ice from different levels of the core at Vostok has allowed the change in temperature and the CO_2 levels over fairly recent times to be estimated. In the chart below the top line indicates the temperature relative to that at the beginning of the industrial revolution. It shows clear glacial periods with warmer interglacial periods between. We are now in one of the latter with the temperature at Vostok 8°C - 10°C higher than it was 20,000 years ago.

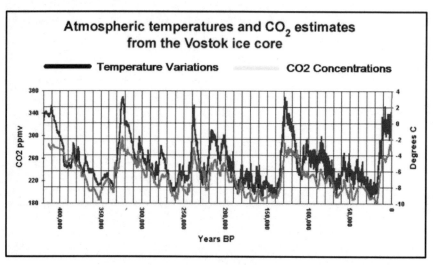

There has been an apparent warming of perhaps 1°C in the last 200 years. This is small but significant in the context of the changes over the last half million years. An increase of another 3°C, which some consider to be a real possibility in the next hundred years, would take the temperature above the highest value recorded over the whole of the period illustrated and it could have a serious impact on the World as we know it. But is it going to happen?

Remember that the Vostok figures shown above were only measured at a single point on the Earth's surface. However, temperature measurements elsewhere in the Antarctic and Greenland show a similar pattern and it is generally accepted that temperatures across the whole planet showed similar fluctuations.

In the past, there was much debate about the cause of the changes but it is now generally accepted that they are caused by the three Milankovich factors which result from periodic changes of the Earth's orbit round the Sun. These cycles, which repeat approximately every 20,000, 40,000 or 100,000 years, sometimes act together and sometimes cancel each other out so that the peaks and troughs in the chart above have a complicated pattern, although it is clear that the 100,000 year cycle dominates.

The process, illustrated below, goes a considerable way towards explaining the changes over the last half million years. A slight shift in the Earth's orbit round the Sun raises the air temperature a little. There is over fifty times more CO_2 dissolved in the oceans than is found in the entire atmosphere and as the sea warms some of the dissolved CO_2 escapes into the atmosphere so the temperature rises more and so on. The two effects reinforce each other and could cause the temperature to go on rising. But so far, it seems that a further shift in the Earth's orbit eventually occurs so that the temperature rise is halted, the interaction between temperature and CO_2 is reversed, and we head towards another glacial period. The change in the Earth's temperature and in CO_2 levels is nothing new. It is important to realise, however, that what certainly is new now **is the speed at which things are changing**.

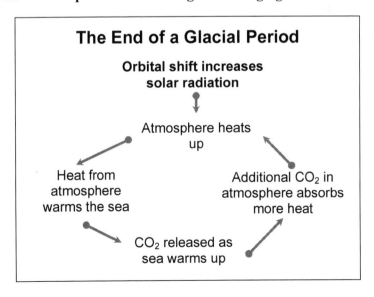

Recent Temperature Changes

The prehistoric temperatures changes, discussed above, are those at a single point on the Earth's surface. Recent changes, over short periods, are smaller and may not be the same everywhere. To see real trends global averages have to be calculated from a range of locations.

There are many historical references to climate and to changes in the climate. Sometimes these compare the current year with earlier years, sometimes they record events such as the freezing of a particular river or lake. In other cases, there is evidence that people were living further up a particular valley because it was warmer than it had been. Such evidence is hard to present in a quantitative form but the idea developed, from historical references, that there had been a medieval warm period (MWP) from 1100 to 1300 and a little ice age (LIA) between 1500 and 1700.

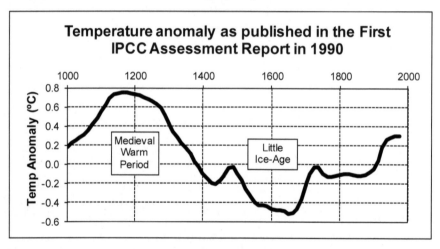

The chart above shows the temperature anomaly over the last 1,000 years as published in the first Intergovernmental Panel on Climate Change (IPCC) Assessment Report in 1990. It clearly shows the MWP and LIA but it is based only on data from the UK and Western Europe since almost all the information available at the time applied only to this region. Since then more data has become available for a variety of other locations spread around the World.

Figures published in 2005 showed the temperature anomaly in seven different regions based on data from ice cores, tree rings, ocean sediments and plant flowering. The next chart shows these figures for each of the seven locations. The new regions show considerably greater variation than was seen in Central England and only partial consistency.

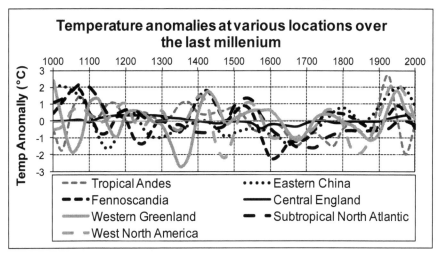

In the next chart, the grey line is the average for the seven locations and most of the differences have been ironed out. The black line is an average figure for many locations in the Northern Hemisphere as published by Mann *et al.* in 1998. This line is based on more widespread information and shows no sign of the MWP and LIA as global phenomena - these are exclusive to Western Europe.

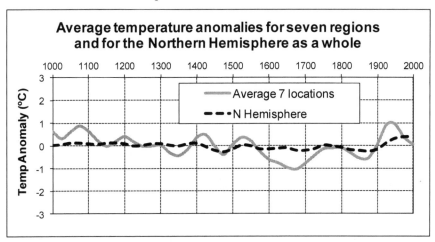

The chart on the next page again shows the estimated change in temperature for the Northern Hemisphere over the last 1,000 years. The figures are similar to those above but have been extended to 2013 and the vertical axis has been expanded relative to the previous chart. The black line shows temperatures relative to the values in 1800 before industrialisation began to have an impact. The grey line shows the "fifty year rolling average" up to 1880 with a 5-year average from then on. This graph is often referred to as the hockey stick.

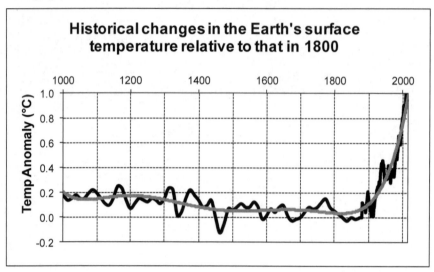

Historical changes in the Earth's surface temperature relative to that in 1800

If we accept that the average temperature was almost constant for eight hundred years and only began to rise with the beginning of the industrial revolution, then, in terms of explaining man's impact on the climate we should concentrate on data gathered for the last 150 years or so. This data is measured instrumentally and has been gathered globally.

The chart on the next page illustrates the data from 1880. The black triangles show the figures for each year with the grey line giving a five-year rolling average. Overall, there is an upward trend but there are still fluctuations from year to year. There were a few volcanoes between 1900 and 1900 after which the temperature began to rise steadily. The drop from 1950 to 1970 is due to an upsurge in volcanoes as well as higher levels of particles produced during the worldwide industrial expansion after the war. There are also little peaks every ten or eleven years which match the varying sunspot cycles. The temperature has risen by about 0.7°C in the last forty years and if this trend continues it will lead to a further rise of at least 2°C in the next hundred years. Remember of course that the figures are averages for the whole globe and much greater changes may be seen at some specific locations but with smaller changes or even decreases at other places.

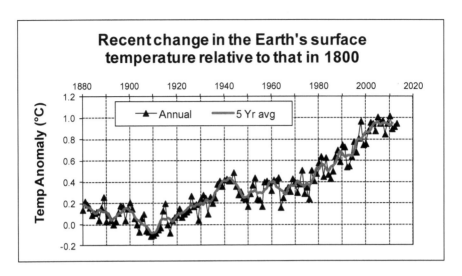

Climate change sceptics often try to discredit the recently measured change in global temperature by talking about the medieval warm period or claiming that there are often new sources of heat adjacent to measuring points. They ignore the fact that it is the average temperature change we are after and there can still be a rise in the average even if there is a fall at one place so long as there is a larger rise elsewhere. There is little doubt that the overall trend is upwards even though there are fluctuations.

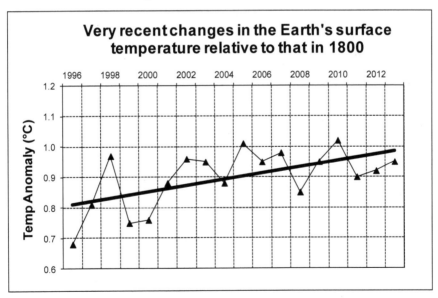

The chart above shows figures for the last 17 years and some have argued that there has been a pause in global warming. From figures for 2005 to

2008 it was argued that the temperature had begun to fall but then the figure for 2009 showed a rise and 2010 was the highest value ever recorded. Although the figure has been slightly lower in the last three years the overall trend over this period is still upward and the argument by a former UK Environment Secretary that the temperature rise has ceased is not realistic.

Sceptics also refer to Climategate and still claim that scientists have been fixing the data even though these challenges have long ago been answered. Recently an independent group of scientists, the Berkeley Group, have reanalysed the data and have come to conclusions almost identical to those published by NOAA (National Oceanographic and Atmospheric Administration) and NASA based on the same data as that used in the graph above.

Modelling The Change

AGW is almost certainly a reality but man's activities are not the only variables. To forecast the future we need a model and this should explain past observations as well as predicting the future. IPCC have developed a model designed to calculate the global temperature. The next chart is based on historical parameters and shows a good match between observed and calculated values up to about 1970, after which the two lines diverge.

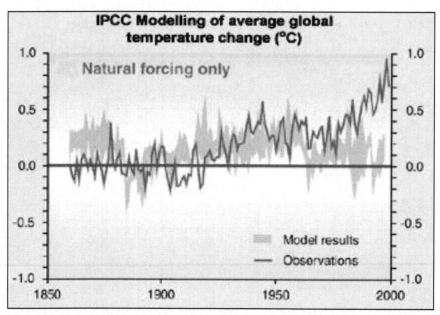

The second chart allows for the impact of anthropogenic factors in addition to historical parameters and the match now continues right through to the present day.

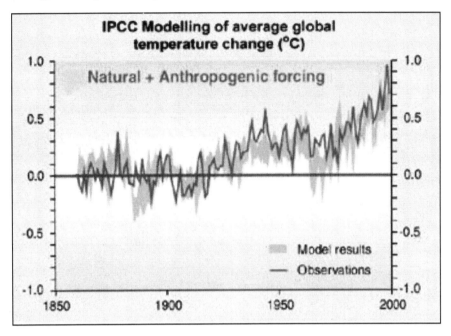

If a model and observations do not match, then clearly the model has faults. The fact that a model and observations do match does not prove that the model is correct but it does suggest that the model is likely to generate reasonable forecasts of the future.

The Carbon Cycle

This section helps you to understand the factors which influence atmospheric CO_2 concentration and how man's activities can affect it.

The total amount of carbon on the Earth is fixed but it exists in a variety of forms and the balance can change with time. Carbon can appear as graphite, graphene or diamond as well as being combined with other elements to form the host of different compounds which are the key components of all living organisms. It also appears in CO_2, both in the atmosphere and dissolved in the oceans. Carbon accounts for about two thirds of the dry weight of all living organisms and is a major component of biomass, the remains of dead and decaying plants and animals, including humus in the soil and sediment on the seabed. Time, temperature and pressure have converted biomass into fossil fuels so that carbon is also the major component of coal, oil and natural gas. There is a complex balance between carbon in its different forms - the diagram illustrates the key elements of the "Carbon Cycle".

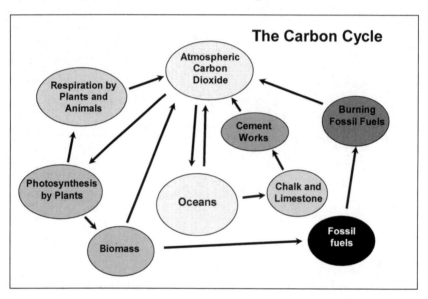

The starting point for the cycle is photosynthesis. Plants absorb CO_2 from the atmosphere and water from the soil. In the process known as photosynthesis, energy from sunlight enables chlorophyll in the leaves to combine these raw materials to make carbohydrates and other substances which are stored in the plant and which help the plant to grow. When these are used by the plant to produce energy the CO_2 is put back into the air although some remains permanently in the plant as protein. When plants die the residue, described as biomass, rots or decays and trees may be burnt putting some of the CO_2 back into the atmosphere.

Many sea creatures have shells of calcium carbonate with the carbon coming from the food they eat. Many generations of shells have accumulated, initially on the seabed, giving rise to limestone and chalk. During the making of cement, when limestone is heated, the CO_2 is put back into the atmosphere.

CO_2 dissolves in water and there is a continuous interchange of the gas between the atmosphere and the surface layer of the oceans with the balance depending on the temperature.

Anything which destroys the land-based reservoirs, particularly burning vegetation or fossil fuels will increase the amount of CO_2 in the atmosphere. Absorption into the oceans or the growing of more trees or other plants is the natural way of reversing this process but it may take many, many years to reach equilibrium.

Methane

Methane, (CH_4), the main constituent of natural gas, is the simplest hydrocarbon. It is also present in the atmosphere although in much smaller quantities than CO_2. Methane, however, is a much more effective GHG than CO_2 and at equal concentrations it would trap at least twenty times as much energy as CO_2 though the exact factor is the subject of disagreement and some would put the ratio higher.

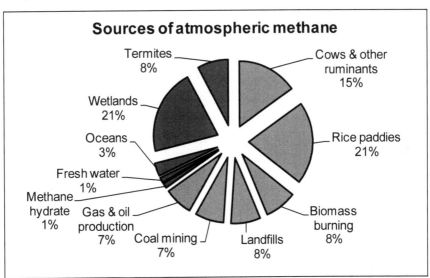

Methane is produced when organic matter decays and rots in a limited supply of air. Ruminants such as cows, sheep and goats generate it in their stomachs and it leaks out from both ends. The diagram above shows the importance of different sources of methane. Two thirds of it, shown by the lighter segments, comes from anthropogenic sources over which man has considerable influence. If methane is allowed to leak into the atmosphere during production of natural gas there is the risk of a considerable increase of CH_4 in the atmosphere.

Once in the atmosphere, methane is oxidised to CO_2 and water and it has an estimated lifetime of about ten years. Because of this short lifespan, the level of methane in the atmosphere soon comes into equilibrium and if we take steps to reduce the output, it will have an effect on the global concentrations within a decade or two. This is very different from the position with CO_2 where the atmospheric concentration will take many thousands of years to reach equilibrium.

Water vapour, CO_2 and methane are the main GHGs. Others include oxides of nitrogen, ozone and CFCs (chlorofluorocarbons).

Levels Of CO_2 And Other GHGs

The most significant GHG in the atmosphere which keeps our temperature well above that on the moon is water and the concentration of this is determined by the equilibrium of water vapour between the atmosphere and the surface of the oceans. This has remained essentially unchanged for hundreds of thousands of years. The level of CO_2 in the atmosphere, however, has changed considerably in the past and has varied from 180 to 300 ppm (parts per million) in the last 600,000 years as shown in the earlier chart on Page 16 - but what has been happening more recently? The chart below shows clearly that the level was almost unchanged for 800 years until the Industrial Revolution. Since 1800 the level has risen by almost half and in 2014, at 400 ppm, it was higher than at any time in the last 600,000 years.

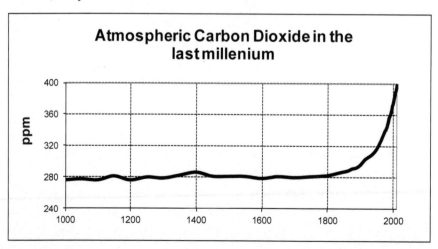

The chart below shows the change over the last 30 years. The increase appears to have been steady at about 1.7 ppm per year. Three quarters of this "anthropogenic" CO_2 is the result of burning fossil fuels while the rest is due to changes in land use, particularly deforestation.

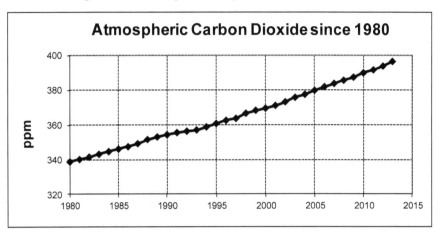

CO_2 is the best-known greenhouse gas but concentrations of methane have more than doubled since 1800 as a result of man's activities. Nitrous oxide, produced in vehicle exhausts and agriculture has increased by 15%.

The adjacent table shows the relative contribution of different GHGs to current anthropogenic temperature rise.

Contribution of GHGs to Global Warming	
Carbon dioxide	53%
Methane	17%
Nitrous Oxide	5%
Ozone	13%
CFCs	12%

Climate Change - Fact Or Fiction?

The words "Climate Change" are often used in the context of gloom as if we have had a perfect climate which has never changed but in fact it has always been changing. In the past, for example, the Sahara desert was green and fertile. As it slowly became more arid people moved, over several generations, to more fertile areas and adapted to the new circumstances. Some more recent examples of "Climate Change" are given on the next page.

Examples of Changes in Climate

- The average surface temperature of the Earth has increased by 0.8°C since 1910. The increase has been fairly steady but with little change between 1945 and 1976. The rate of increase is now about 2°C per 100 years. It appears to be continuing and this rate is probably accelerating.

- The 1990s were the warmest decade of the millennium and 1998 the warmest year until 2005. After this there was a slight drop but the average in 2010 was back up to the 2005 figure.

- Over land the minimum night time temperature increased by about 1°C between 1900 and 2000 thus extending the freeze free period in many regions. During the same period the increase in maximum daytime temperature was only 0.5°C - and over the sea it was even less.

- Satellite data show that snow and ice cover has decreased by 10% since the 1960s including a retreat of mountain glaciers. Rivers and lakes in the mid and high latitudes of the Northern Hemisphere now remain frozen for two to three weeks less than in 1900.

- Spring and summer sea ice in the Northern hemisphere has declined by 10-15% since the 1950s.

- Average sea levels rose by between 10 cm and 20 cm during the 1900s and are currently rising at about 3mm per year.

- Since sub surface measurements have become available it is apparent that the overall temperature of the oceans has increased since the 1950s.

- During the 1900s rainfall has increased in the Northern Hemisphere by 5-10% in mid and high latitudes and 2-3% in the tropics. It has decreased by about 3% in the sub tropics between 10°N and 30°N.

- Since 1950 there has been a small increase in heavy rain and snow storms.

- In the Northern mid and to high latitudes there was an increase of 2% in cloud cover leading to a narrowing of the range between maximum and minimum temperatures during the 1900s.

- El Niño events result from Westerly winds blowing across the Pacific and building water up against the West coast of South America. When these winds cease the water flows back again creating these events which have been more frequent since the 1970s than in the previous 100 years.

- There has been some increase in periods of extreme drought and extreme wetness, particularly in parts of Africa and Asia.

- The amount of spring rain in Ethiopia and Niger has reduced steadily since 1996 as a result of the rising temperature of the surface of the Indian Ocean. This puts 10 million people at risk of starvation.

The climate we have now is the one we are used to and if it changes we will have to adapt to it. There is little doubt that Global Warming has been taking place for the last 200 years during which time the temperature has increased by almost 1°C. The increase over the last 30 years, at a rate of 2°C per century, is about ten times faster than at any time in the last half million years. The potential problem arises because the climate is now changing quickly so we need to adapt quickly and we may not be able to move fast enough. What we need to do is to **predict** what is likely to happen and then to identify where man can **deliberately intervene**.

A rise of 1°C in the average does not sound like a major problem when many places vary by 40°C between winter and summer. However, the small change can be enough to disturb the complex patterns in the airflows and ocean currents in a way that can create significant local Climate Change. In addition, we need to be wary of averages since the changes are not the same everywhere. Not everyone agrees about the extent to which the climate has changed but the consensus now is that there have been changes.

The box on the previous page lists some of the small, but definite changes, which have been observed. Some of the changes (e.g. more rainfall or a narrower temperature range) might well be regarded as beneficial. Many of the conclusions relate to the Northern Hemisphere. This is not because there have been more changes here than in the Southern Hemisphere but, since there are more observations, conclusions can be reached more easily.

Overall, the changes listed above may look quite modest but often they are concentrated locally. If you were at the centre of the developing droughts in Ethiopia or Niger, you would not consider the changes minor. Similarly, rising sea levels can be disastrous for those living close to the coast. Ten million people in Bangladesh and another 25 million in southern China live less than a metre above sea level. Hurricane Katrina was not a modest affair for those in New Orleans.

We now have a fair idea of where we are as a result of a temperature rise of 1°C in the last two hundred years. The rest of the book is devoted to where we might be heading and the extent to which we may be able to control the temperature rise and deal with its consequences.

Chapter 4

Fossil Fuels – History And Use

The Industrial Revolution

Until 10,000 years ago man's only source of mechanical energy, for digging fields or grinding corn were his own muscles but then he began to harness animals. Later on windmills and waterpower came into use but not until 1750 was their size sufficient to have more than local impact when waterpower began to find use in sawmills, textiles factories and in papermaking. This was the start of the Industrial Revolution.

Iron had been produced by many societies since the beginning of the Iron Age but the quantities were small and smelting relied on charcoal made from trees. In 1709 Abraham Darby began converting coal into a coke that could be used as a cheap alternative to charcoal. From 1750 large scale production of iron began and consumption of fossil fuels took off. In 1769, James Watt patented the first steam engine adding further impetus to demand for fuel although it was not until the middle of the eighteen hundreds that the output of coal powered steam engines exceeded that of water mills.

Steam engines have the advantage of mobility on land and sea and thus began our love affair with travel. As we moved into the nineteen hundreds coal began to be replaced by oil and then, after another 50 years, natural gas entered the field.

Where Fossil Fuels Came From

The main raw materials for plants are CO_2, absorbed through the leaves and water, from the roots. In the process of photosynthesis, plants store energy from the sunlight falling on their leaves by converting these raw materials into carbohydrates and other organic chemicals.

In the carboniferous era, 350 million years ago, small unicellular plants and animals feeding on them grew in the oceans. When they died, they sank to the seabed building up layers of "biomass". Minerals then deposited on them trapping the organic debris in layers of rock. Further layers of biomass from more complex plants also built up in bogs and marshland. Geological movement buried some of these materials deep underground where, under the influence of heat flowing up from the Earth's core, combined with high pressures, the biomass was converted into fossil fuels. Most of these are deeply buried and oil has been found as much as 6 km below the surface. Coal, however, is sometimes found near the Earth's surface and is often accessible from opencast mines. Natural gas is frequently associated with oil and it is sometimes present in large quantities in shale from which it can be extracted by fracking.

The composition of fossil fuels varies widely depending on the conditions which produced them. They range from natural gas with four hydrogen atoms for each carbon atom to anthracite which is almost pure carbon. In between are light and heavy crude oils and various grades of bituminous coal. Across this range, is a decreasing ratio of hydrogen to carbon.

TOE - Tonnes of Oil Equivalent

If you burn a tonne of coal you release a certain amount of energy. Burning a tonne of oil releases about 50% more energy. To make the comparison of different fuels easier, quantities of energy are often expressed as "tonnes of oil equivalent" or TOE. Not all fuels have the same amount of energy per unit weight but one TOE (the amount of energy released by burning 1 tonne of oil) has been standardised as 10,034 megacalories for any fuel.

Throughout this book the quantity of energy, including that from fossil fuels and from renewables is, for ease of comparison, usually expressed in TOE or in multiples such as BTOE (billions of tonnes of oil equivalent).

Why Fossil Fuels Are Harmful

When we burn fossil fuels we release energy absorbed in the past and at the same time, we put back into the atmosphere the CO_2 which was absorbed from it all those years ago. The fossil fuels took many millions of years to form but we will quite likely consume most of the reserves and release the associated CO_2 in less than four hundred years.

Burning 1 TOE of any fossil fuel will release the same amount of energy as burning a tonne of oil but burning coal release more CO_2 than burning the amount oil or gas required to give the same amount of energy. The chart on the next page shows the differing amounts of actual fuel consumed and the CO_2 released when one TOE of coal, oil or gas is burned. The figures, particularly for coal, are not exact and vary with the grade of fuel.

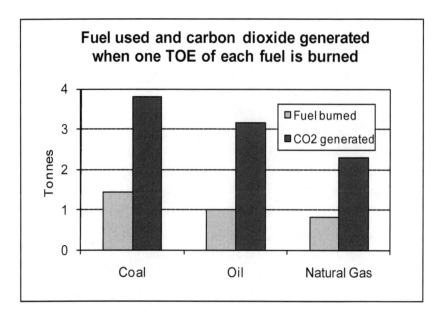

Of the CO_2 put into the atmosphere about a quarter is absorbed by the land and a similar amount by the oceans. This reduces the build up in the atmosphere, but it makes the oceans more acidic leading to things such as the disintegration of coral reefs. Half of the CO_2 remains in the air and this has caused levels to rise from 280 ppm in 1800 to the current level of 400 ppm as discussed earlier. This is what, in a large part, has set in motion the recent accelerating rise in the Earth's temperature.

Biofuels are made from plants. When they are used as fuel the amount of CO_2 released is the same as that absorbed when they were grown but this CO_2 will be reabsorbed when replacement crops are grown. So long as replacements are grown, burning biomass has no net effect on atmospheric levels of CO_2. Such fuels are said to be carbon neutral but remember this is only true as long as the plants being burned are being replaced. Clearing Brazilian rain forests and burning the trees, without growing replacements is certainly not carbon neutral.

Uncertainties

The figures relating to production and consumption of fossil fuels used below come from statistics gathered by the United Nations or by BP. They all rely on data from individual countries or companies which may use different methods of calculation. There may also be political or economic factors which affect the reporting of values. This accounts for some of the year to year fluctuations seen in the figures although other variations may be the result of major world events such as the Gulf War or economic recessions.

Fossil Fuels And Who Produces Them

Fossil fuel consumption has increased dramatically since coal mining began seriously. Since 1900, overall consumption has increased by a factor of 26 while the global population has increased by a factor of less than 5. Per capita consumption worldwide has thus increased by a factor of more than five since 1900.

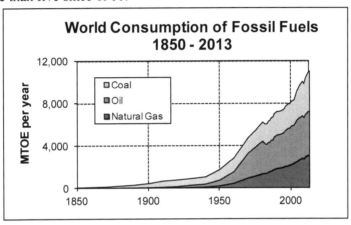

- Coal

Significant coal production began in the early eighteen hundreds. From almost nothing it had reached almost 400 million TOE a year by 1900 and in the next 50 years it more than doubled to 1 billion TOE. By now the figure has increased a further four times to almost 4 billion TOE a year – more than half a tonne per year of coal for every one of us on the planet.

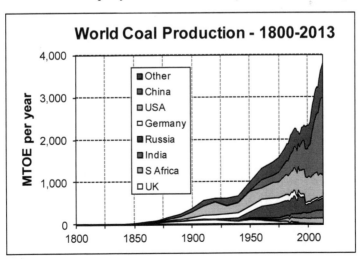

Today's coal production is dominated by two countries, China and the USA which account for over 60% of total production. Most of the rest comes from only another 10 countries. In 1900, UK production was 30% of the World total, in 1980 it was down to 4%, but it has now fallen dramatically to only 0.3%.

Shares Of World Coal Production - 2013					
China	47.6%	Russia	4.3%	Ukraine	1.2%
USA	12.9%	South Africa	3.7%	Germany	1.1%
Australia	6.9%	Kazakhstan	1.5%	Canada	0.9%
Indonesia	6.7%	Poland	1.5%	UK	0.3%
India	5.9%	Colombia	1.4%	The Rest	4.3%

- Oil

Colonel Drake is credited with drilling the first oil well in Pennsylvania in 1859 although some wells may have been drilled in West Virginia in the 1820s. Initially growth was small and by 1900 almost twenty times more coal than oil was still produced worldwide in terms of TOE. It was not until 1963 that oil production exceeded that of coal. The industry remained dominated by the USA for many years and in 1940, they still accounted for 70% of production.

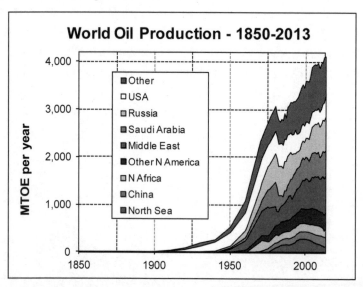

Currently the shares of the three leading producers, Saudi Arabia, Russia and the USA are around 10% each with the rest of the Middle East accounting for a similar amount. There are more than twenty countries which individually contribute 1% or more of the total.

Shares of World Oil Production - 2013							
Saudi Arabia	13.1%	Kuwait	3.7%	Norway	2.0%	Oman	1.1%
Russia	12.9%	Iraq	3.7%	Kazakhstan	2.0%	Libya	1.1%
USA	10.8%	Mexico	3.4%	Qatar	2.0%	India	1.0%
China	5.0%	Venezuela	3.3%	Algeria	1.7%	UK	1.0%
Canada	4.7%	Nigeria	2.7%	Azerbaijan	1.3%		
Iran	4.0%	Brazil	2.7%	Colombia	1.3%		
UAE	4.0%	Angola	2.1%	Indonesia	1.1%	The Rest	8.5%

- Natural Gas

Natural gas production began in the USA in about 1900 and grew slowly until by 1950 it still accounted for only 10% fossil fuel production. Most of this was produced in the USA. Natural gas now accounts for more than a quarter of all the fossil fuels produced.

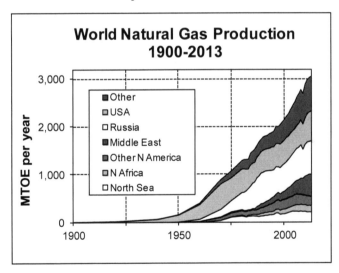

Currently almost half of gas production is in North America or Russia but there are many other significant players. Recent discoveries of shale oil gas may change the picture in the future with possible widespread introduction of fracking. Production of shale oil gas with fracking raises a number of environmental questions including the possible leakage of methane into the atmosphere, contamination of water supplies and the initiation of earthquakes though there is so far little evidence of these problems.

Shares of World Gas Production - 2013									
USA	20.5%	Saudi Arabia	3.0%	Mexico	1.7%	Pakistan	1.1%
Russia	17.8%	Algeria	2.3%	UK	1.7%	Nigeria	1.1%
Iran	4.9%	Indonesia	2.1%	Uzbekistan	1.6%	Argentina	1.0%
Qatar	4.7%	Netherlands	2.0%	UAE	1.6%	India	1.0%
Canada	4.6%	Malaysia	2.0%	Australia	1.3%		
China	3.4%	Egypt	1.9%	Trin & Tob	1.3%		
Norway	3.2%	Turkmenistan	1.8%	Thailand	1.2%	The Rest	11.6%

- Total Production

The next chart shows the major overall producers of fossil fuels in 2013. The top four countries account for almost half the World's current production. In the future, as fossil fuels become more scarce, major producers will have very considerable political and economic power unless we develop renewable alternatives which everyone can produce for themselves.

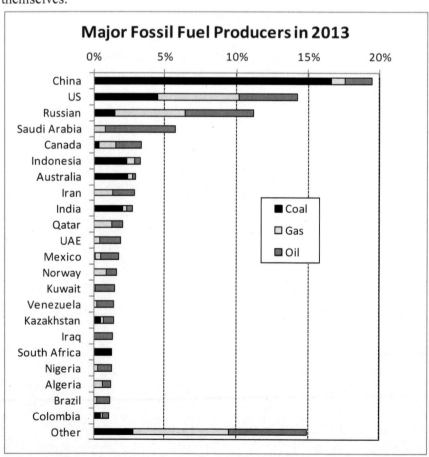

How Long Will Reserves Last?

We have talked about how fossil fuels were formed and how much we have used so far. Although reserves are finite it is not easy to work out with certainty how long they will last. Data is available on "Proven Reserves" - this is the total amount of fuel which could be produced economically from known reserves at the present time. Proven reserves are likely to be an under estimate for two reasons. Firstly as reserves become more scarce the price will rise and a greater proportion of them will then become economically recoverable, at least in the short-term, and secondly it is likely that more reserves will be discovered.

The worldwide proven reserves of oil now stands at around 190 BTOE and we are using it up at a rate of nearly 4 billion TOE a year. The ratio of reserves divided by production, often referred to as the R/P ratio, is thus approaching 50. If the World continues using oil at the present rate and we don't discover any more, then it will not be long before we run out. The table shows details for major world regions. In practice, of course, rates of consumption will increase in the short-term so reserves will in reality run out more quickly than the R/P ratio suggests.

Proven Reserves and Production of Oil - 2013		
	Proven Res'ves	Annual Prod'n	R/P
Middle East	47.9%	32.2%	78
S. America	19.5%	9.1%	100
Africa	7.7%	10.1%	40
Eurasia	8.8%	20.3%	23
N. America	13.6%	18.9%	37
Asia/Pacific	2.5%	9.5%	14
World	100.0%	100.0%	46

These figures cover conventional oil reserves but there are possible "unconventional" sources which include very heavy oil in the Orinoco Valley in Venezuela and the Athabasca tar sands in Canada as well as Oil Shale in the USA, in Estonia, Russia, Brazil, the UK and China. Some estimates put the total unconventional reserves at three or four times the amount of "proven" reserves but exploitation of them may well have very adverse environmental consequences, both locally and globally.

Similar calculations can be carried out for natural gas and coal and the next two tables show the regional distribution of these reserves and the R/P ratios. The picture for gas and coal production is very different from that for oil. Russia is the leading producer of gas accounting for 20% of World output most of which is exported. The USA accounts for almost as much but all of it is consumed at home. However, the USA, with only 3% of reserves will be needing alternative supplies in the near future although fracking and recent new discoveries are currently relieving some of the pressure.

As we saw earlier coal was by far the most important fossil fuel well into the nineteen hundreds and it was not until the early 1960s that it was overtaken by oil. Coal now accounts for 30% of the World's fossil fuel consumption and there are indications that it may become more important again. At current rates of consumption reserves will last another 120 years. In terms of supply there is no currently pressing problem.

Proven Reserves & Production of Natural Gas - 2013					Proven Reserves & Production of Coal - 2013			
	Proven Res'ves	Ann Prod'n	R/P			Proven Res'ves	Ann Prod'n	R/P
Middle East	43.2%	16.7%	100		Asia/Pacific	32.3%	68.9%	54
Eurasia	30.5%	31.0%	54		Eurasia	34.8%	11.6%	250
Asia/Pacific	8.2%	14.4%	31		N. America	27.5%	14.1%	250
Africa	7.6%	6.0%	70		Africa	3.7%	3.8%	130
N. America	6.3%	26.7%	13		S. America	1.6%	1.6%	150
S. America	4.1%	5.2%	44		World	100.0%	100.0%	120
Total	100.0%	100.0%	60					

Overall Reserves

Based on proven reserves and current production rates we have enough oil for 45 years, enough gas for 60 years and enough coal for 120 years. Combining reserves and consumption of all fossil fuels, the R/P ratio is about 75 years. The figures are based on proven reserves but as mentioned earlier the figures are not set in stone. There are other undiscovered reserves but it goes without saying that, until such reserves have been found, we cannot put an accurate value on the amount. In addition there are known reserves of shale gas, tar sands and other types of very heavy oil which are not usually included in the proven reserves total.

Although the fossil fuels will not run out in my lifetime we are likely to see significant prices rises in the next twenty years and my grandchildren will feel the pinch. Despite the recent fall in the price of oil, future rises are inevitable as reserves are depleted. The temporary drop in price will make it harder for renewables to be competitive but in the end they must compete even if substantial subsidies are necessary. As mentioned earlier some people suggest that the amount of fossil fuels waiting to be discovered may be as much as four times the current proven reserves. If this is true then we will run out of fossil fuels not in 75 years, but in perhaps 300 years at the present rate of consumption. See Chapter 9 for more detail on this.

However, burning all the proven reserves, let alone reserves not yet discovered could have a very serious impact on Global Warming. Burning all the current proven reserves of fossil fuels would more than double the current level of CO_2 in the atmosphere. Burning as yet unproven reserves would have an even greater impact and could increase CO_2 in the atmosphere by a factor approaching 10. This would have a disastrous impact on the climate.

Chapter 5

How We Use Energy

Our use of energy can be classified under the following main headings:

- heating
- lighting
- transport
- electrical and electronic devices
- manufacturing.

Most of the energy we use now comes from fossil fuels although around 15% of the total comes from carbon neutral energy sources including biomass, hydroelectricity or nuclear power with a little from geothermal, wind, solar or wave sources. In order to control Climate Change we eventually need to eliminate all use of fossil fuels. There are three ways we can move in this direction:

- using energy more efficiently while undertaking the same activities
- replacing fossil fuels with energy from renewable, carbon neutral, sources.
- cutting down on energy-consuming activities.

Efficiency

The most obvious way of reducing energy consumption is to use less energy while reaching the same result. This can be achieved by improving efficiency. Efficiency makes sure that as much energy as possible ends up where we want it with as little as possible merely "going up in smoke".

In the main we want energy to end up as heat, light or motion and any of these may involve electricity. Sometimes the route from source to end use is very simple, in other cases it is more complicated and less efficient.

Every application of energy involves some process of converting the energy stored in the fuel or other source into a form appropriate to the application involved. To the unconcerned end-user it is the final product that matters and if, for example, electricity is needed it doesn't matter to them how that electricity was generated. However, if you are concerned about the environment then, of course, how it was generated does matter.

The Carnot Cycle

The maximum attainable efficiency whenever we convert heat into mechanical power is always well below 100% and this maximum can be calculated using Carnot's theorem. The Carnot efficiency is a result of fundamental physics and there is no way in which a machine can be more efficient than this. If steam goes into a turbine at 500°C and comes out of the exhaust at 150°C the maximum efficiency of the generator, according to Carnot, is 45% - over half the energy put in is unavoidably lost. If the input temperature is raised to 700°C then the theoretical efficiency is somewhat better but is still only 57%.

In practice the situation is always worse than these figures suggest. Some heat is lost up the boiler chimney and there are other losses from friction as well as in the power distribution system. These additional losses further reduce the efficiency with which the energy from fossil fuels is converted into useful mechanical energy or electricity. Similar considerations apply to all "heat engines". These include petrol and diesel engines and gas turbines as well as steam engines, all of which are used to convert heat into mechanical energy. In practice the efficiency of good modern electricity generators is about 38%.

On the plus side, some of the "waste" heat can sometimes be recovered and put to good use. For example, in a combined heat and power plant electricity is produced and the warm steam leaving the turbine is used to provide heating via a district system.

Carbon Dioxide From Fossil Fuels

Burning any fossil fuel releases some CO_2 and about half of it remains in the atmosphere. It is this half which has set in motion the steady rise in the Earth's temperature and with it Climate Change. Of the fossil fuels used, natural gas, as we saw earlier is the cleanest. For the same amount of energy, oil puts 40% more CO_2 into the atmosphere while coal releases 70% more. One way of reducing CO_2 emissions would be to get more of our energy from gas rather than from coal. The trend, however, is moving in the opposite direction in some countries, driven by the ready availability of coal and the decline in gas reserves.

Another way of reducing the amount of CO_2 released into the atmosphere is carbon capture and storage (CCS) or carbon sequestration. The CO_2 is extracted from the flue gases of large power stations and then stored in underground reservoirs or in the depths of the oceans. The possibilities of CCS are being explored but there are no systems of significant size anywhere near completion and CCS is probably a distraction from the main issue. What we really need to do is eliminate all use of fossil fuels as they will eventually run out.

Carbon Neutral

We can also reduce the total amount of CO_2 released by using carbon neutral energy. This is either:

- energy from a source where no CO_2 is involved either during production or use
- or where the CO_2 released into the atmosphere when the fuel is used is cancelled out by an equal amount of gas which is absorbed during production of the next batch of fuel.

Under the first category are solar power, hydroelectricity, geothermal energy and nuclear power as well as electricity from wind, waves and tide. Biofuels, where CO_2 is absorbed when growing next year's fuel, are in the second category.

In practice, however, none of them are at present 100% carbon neutral. A certain amount of fossil fuel is currently used to build the production plant and run them or to plant, fertilize and harvest the crops. When the fossil fuels used for these purposes are replaced by other carbon neutral fuels then the overall process will itself become carbon neutral.

Some plants, such as soya, sugar cane or switch grass, can be grown specifically to produce fuels with production and consumption occurring within a short space of time. However, clearing forests, which have been growing for hundreds of years will initially put large amounts of CO_2 into the atmosphere when the timber is burned and it can take many years for this to be cancelled out by the regrowth of trees. In many cases forests are merely cleared and the land used for some other purpose and there is no regrowth. This is certainly not a carbon neutral activity.

Renewable Energy

Fossil fuels are not renewable because supplies are finite and when they have been used once, they are gone. However most "carbon neutral" energy is "renewable" because supplies are effectively unlimited.

Electricity from photoelectric cells or hot water from solar panels are renewable as they rely on energy from the Sun. Wave and wind power are consequences of the weather driven by the Sun and biofuels are produced from crops which grow through absorption of the sunlight. The tides are the result of the gravitational interaction between the Sun, the Moon and the Earth's rotation. Geothermal energy is not strictly renewable but the quantity of energy stored in the Earth's core is so huge that it is effectively infinite. Nuclear power is also not strictly renewable at present as it relies on minerals which are only available in finite amounts. I have, however, included nuclear with renewables as it is carbon neutral. Furthermore the situation would be very different if nuclear fusion processes, for which the raw materials are available in huge amounts, could be developed.

Harvesting Trees

Cutting down and burning the rain forests in Brazil is anything but carbon neutral. As the trees are burned the carbon in the timber, absorbed over hundreds of years, is released as CO_2 and the energy from the combustion is often not put to good use. The crops which replace the trees absorb a little CO_2 as they grow but the volume is tiny compared to that released when the trees are burned.

Harvesting timber from forests in, for example, Finland is usually regarded as carbon neutral as the forests are replanted. If the trees have been burned as fuel, an equivalent amount CO_2 will be absorbed as the new trees grow.

Burning timber as a fuel is only carbon neutral if the volume of timber in forests worldwide is unchanged. If a forest is cleared and not replanted, the burning of the timber is certainly not a carbon neutral process. Furthermore the planting of these replacement trees **should not be considered as part of some offsetting scheme** - their planting is already offsetting the CO_2 released when the original trees were burned in the first place.

Carbon Dioxide And Electricity

A great deal of the energy we use is known as primary energy. This is where the fuel is used directly as when we burn gas to do our cooking or use fuel in cars. We also use a great deal of electricity. Much of this is so-called secondary energy because it is generated by burning fossil fuels in power stations and the original energy in the fuel is only used indirectly. Some electricity is classified as primary because it is made without using fossil fuels. Primary electricity includes hydro, nuclear, geothermal, solar, wind, wave and tidal power.

The carbon footprint of electricity from different sources can be compared by calculating the amount of CO_2 produced for every kWh of electricity generated. The largest source of CO_2 is the fossil fuel used to generate secondary electricity. However, additional fossil fuel is associated with the building, maintenance and decommissioning of both primary and secondary plant and in some cases with the growing of biofuel. These all contribute to the lifetime footprint of electricity from each of the sources.

Carbon Footprint

The term "carbon footprint" is widely used. It is a measure of the amount of carbon dioxide released during a particular process or by a region, a country or an individual. In this case it can be expressed as the grams of CO_2 released when 1 kWh (1 unit) of electricity is generated.

Contributions to the footprint also come from the energy used to mine the coal and transport it to the power station, drill for gas and build the pipelines or refine the oil. Further energy is used to grind coal or run pumps. With a nuclear power station fossil fuels are used in building the plant and mining and processing of nuclear fuel. Fossil fuels are also consumed in the growing of biofuels, in the drilling required to produce geothermal power or in the manufacture and installation of wind turbines.

A comparison of the total CO_2 released during generation of secondary electricity from different fuels and in various primary processes is shown in the table, after taking into account all the additional sources of CO_2. The figures show very clearly that the CO_2 produced during generation of secondary electricity is much greater than for primary power, with coal showing by far the largest footprint.

Carbon Footprint from different Electricity sources

"Fuel"	g CO_2/kWh
Coal	1,100
Oil	650
Gas	400
Geothermal	80
Photovoltaic - UK	58
Photovoltaic - S Europe	35
Wave/Tidal	25-50
Woodchip	25
Hydro	5-30
Wind	5
Nuclear	5

Most of the primary electricity currently produced is hydro or nuclear and both of these have low footprints. Other forms of primary electricity, wind or wave power or photovoltaic electricity also have low footprints and these sources will grow in importance. In the future as more energy comes from carbon neutral sources the amount of CO_2 associated with primary electricity will fall eventually dropping to zero, if and when we cease burning fossil fuels.

Electricity In Different Countries

The footprint of the electricity I consume in the UK depends on the average for the country as a whole. At present 35% of our electricity comes from coal-powered stations, about 40% from gas but only 1% from oil. 16% comes from nuclear and about 8% from other renewables. On average we produce 550g of CO_2 per unit of electricity. If we increase the proportion of nuclear power then the average will fall while if we were to build more coal-fired stations the average would go up.

In a particular country electricity from all the different sources is fed into the grid. The mix of electricity sources varies from country to country and with it the average electricity footprint. The table shows the average footprint in various countries. In France with a high proportion of nuclear power the figure is less than 100 g per kilowatt-hour while in China where over half of electricity currently comes from coal the figure is much more, heading towards 800g.

Carbon footprint from electricity in different countries	
	g CO_2/kWh
France	80
Finland	240
UK	550
USA	610
China	760

Electricity Versus Fossil Fuels

Petrol engines can have an efficiency of 35% when operating at full power but overall, taking into account idling and so forth, only about 20% of the energy in the fuel is converted into useful mechanical energy. Diesel can have a maximum efficiency of over 50% but in practice the overall efficiency is about 30%. Well over half the energy we put into most engines is lost.

The relative impact of different forms of energy on the environment depends on the particular circumstances. If you use gas to heat your house you release 260 g CO_2 for every kWh of useful heat. If you use UK electricity then you will release 550 g CO_2 for the same result. If you were using electricity in France then the figure would be less than 100g/kWh. Now put a PV panel on your roof and use this for your heating, then for every kWh of heating you release only about 60 g CO_2, after allowing for the CO_2 produced when making and installing the panel. Similar arguments can be applied to many other applications.

Suppose you have a small diesel car. On average this is likely to release about 110g CO_2 per km. A similar sized electric car will release 80-90 g CO_2/km, assuming average UK electricity is used to recharge the batteries. Electric cars are often said to be much cleaner than their petrol or diesel brothers, but this is only true at street level. Electric cars are often cheaper to run but this is because the tax charged on motor fuel is not applied to the fuel used to generate electricity. This leads to spurious comparisons of their efficiency, based on the cost to the end-user rather than on the amount of CO_2 produced.

Like electricity, hydrogen is sometimes promoted as a clean fuel for vehicles. Again it is clean at street level but it is a secondary fuel. It can be made by heating fossil fuels or biomass or by the electrolysis of water. Its overall cleanliness depends on the source of the heat or on how the electricity used was generated. If all the power came from a hydro station or a wind turbine then it would be very clean but if it had been produced in a coal burning facility, it would be anything but clean. This issue is discussed in more detail in Chapter 10.

Chapter 6

Carbon Footprints

What Is A Footprint?

A "Carbon Footprint" measures the net amount of CO_2 an individual, a group of people, an organisation or a nation release into the atmosphere. Carbon footprints can also relate to a particular product or activity. Other greenhouse gases can be included in the footprint by calculating their CO_2 equivalent or CO_2e. This is the quantity of the gas concerned multiplied by its impact as a GHG relative to CO_2. In general inclusion of GHGs other than CO_2 increases the carbon foot print by about 10-20%. Unless otherwise mentioned the data below relates to CO_2 rather than to CO_2e.

Based on the fossil fuels consumed worldwide, the global carbon footprint was about 35 billion tonnes in 2013, up almost 7% since 2010. The chart below shows the major contributors to this, based on the quantity of fossil fuels consumed in each country. In total, Developed and Industrialised Countries, with only 20% of World population, account for 45% of the global footprint. Details of how countries are classified are given in Appendix A.

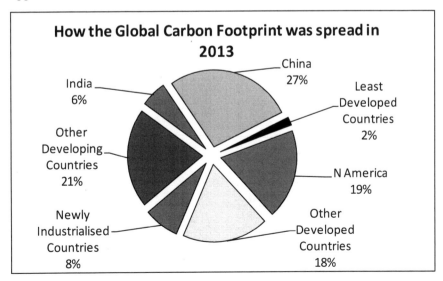

How the Global Carbon Footprint was spread in 2013

China 27%

Least Developed Countries 2%

N America 19%

Other Developed Countries 18%

Newly Industrialised Countries 8%

Other Developing Countries 21%

India 6%

Footprints are often presented as a per capita value. This is the total footprint for a country divided by its population and allows more meaningful comparison of countries or regions. The next chart shows the per capita footprint in a selection of countries or regions chosen to illustrate the important differences. It must, however, be remembered that these figures are based on fossil fuel consumption within the region. The true footprint in most Developed countries is actually higher but in, for example, China it is lower. These differences arise from the footprint associated with products made in one country and exported to another.

Figures are shown for 2005, 2010 and 2013. On average each inhabitant of the planet generates nearly five tonnes of CO_2 per year with an increase of 10% between 2005 and 2013. The USA is top of the list with an average footprint of almost 22 tonnes per person in 2005 falling back to about 19 tonnes in 2013. At the other end of the scale is Bangladesh with a footprint of only 0.3 tonnes per person in 2005 rising to 0.4 in 2013 – fifty times less than in the USA.

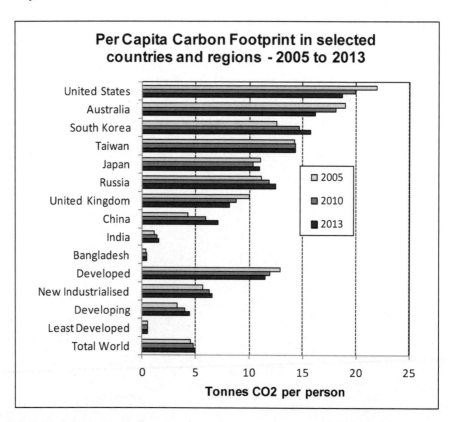

There has been a fall in a number of Developed Countries similar to that in the USA. The decrease may be the result of concern over Climate Change but it is more likely to be a consequence of the recent economic problems and the increase of imports, particularly from China. The figure for China, on the other hand, has been increasing, partly because of exports, and it is now above the World average. India, at only 1 tonne, is much lower though still substantially above Bangladesh. The average footprint for all Developed Countries in 2013 was about 11.5 tonnes per person showing a slight fall since 2005. In the Newly Industrialised Countries the figure is about half of this but it is showing an increase and levels are likely to merge in the longer term with Developed Countries. In Developing Countries the footprint is much lower and in 2005 it was only 25% of that in Developed Countries. However, the level is increasing and by 2013 it was up to almost 40% of the Developed Country level with much of the increase coming from China, partly as a result of its exports. The figure in the Least Developed Counties remains very low at only 4% of the average for the Rich World. In reality the difference between Rich and Poor is actually greater because the footprint of goods we in the Developed World import from Developing Countries really adds to our own footprint while subtracting from theirs.

Remember that the numbers above are per capita figures so any drop in the footprint may be offset by an increase in population, so the overall level of emissions may increase more than the average per capita figure.

The chart on the next page shows the percentage changes in total footprints. Overall Developed Countries have shown a small drop. The UK has apparently done very well with a decrease between 2005 and 2013 of 17% and an overall decrease since 1990 of 25%. Part of this decrease is the result of less manufacturing at home and more imports, particularly from China. The USA has also shown a decrease partly due to the economic problems and more imports but also because of increasing use of natural gas from fracking. Some Developed Countries have shown an increase, notably Australia and South Korea. Developing countries have shown an increase of over 40% led by China. Even in the Least Developed Countries the overall footprint has increased by over 20%, partly as a result of increasing population. It is sometimes claimed that cooking in the LDCs has a serious impact on CO_2 emissions but this ignores the fact that most of the fuel used is biomass and the CO_2 is reabsorbed as the next batch of biomass is grown.

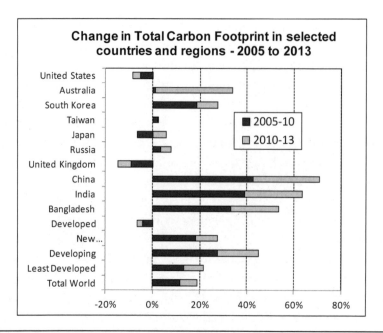

Carbs
Burning of fossil fuels in the UK releases approximately 8.5 tonnes, or 8,500 kg, a year of CO_2 for each citizen. To simplify the text below I refer to the UK footprint in terms of "carbs" where 1 carb equals 1 kg of CO_2.

The UK Footprint

As an example of how different components contribute to an individual footprint I have looked in some detail at the UK, where the average footprint is 8.5 tonnes of CO_2 (8,500 Carbs) per year excluding any effect of imports. The chart below shows how emissions in the UK in 2013 were divided between the four sectors each of which I will discuss in turn.

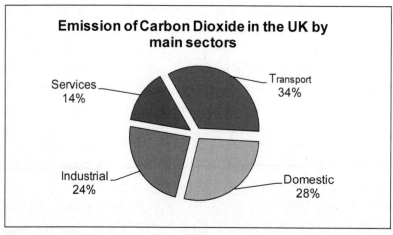

The Footprint Of Our Homes

The next chart shows that half of our domestic footprint in 2013 (14% of the total) came from space heating, about a quarter of it from water heating, with the rest coming from cooking and the use of an assortment of electrical equipment.

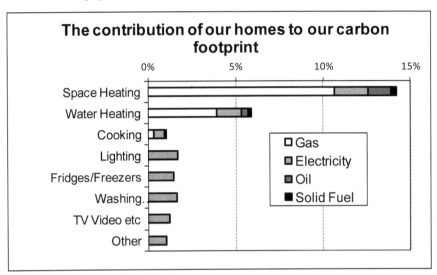

– Space Heating

What we individually produce depends on the type of house we live in and what temperature we choose to live at. Since the 1970s we have more than halved the amount of energy used for space heating. **Make sure that you**:

- have a gas boiler with efficiency in the range 80-90% – boilers much more than 6 years old are unlikely to be this efficient
- fill the cavity in cavity walls with foam or add surface insulation inside or out if you don't have cavity walls
- double glaze all windows – or even use triple glazing
- insulate your attic with at least 250mm of insulation
- reduce room temperature from 20°C to 18°C for day time and to 15°C at night, install thermostatic radiators valves in every room
- eliminate all drafts.

In the table on the next page "As it was" is how most houses were in the 1970's and how some still are. "As it is now" shows what many people have done since then but most of us have not implemented all the options. Few of us have moved to "As it could be" and indeed if we did there would be a shortage of woodchips!

	As it was	As it is now	As it could be
Boiler efficiency	60%	90%	90%
Wall insulation	No	Yes	Yes
Window glazing/frames	single - metal	double	triple - argon
Loft insulation	100 mm	250 mm	400 mm
Thermostatic Rad. Valves	No	Some	All
Day temperature	20°C	20°C	18°C
Night temperature	20°C	20°C	15°C
Air changes per hour	2	0.5	0.5
Carbs per person	4,700	1,350	850
Relative CO_2 emissions	250%	100%	60%
Woodchip boiler	No	No	Yes
CO_2 with Woodchip boiler	250%	100%	10%

– Hot Water

Domestic hot water is usually supplied either from a hot water cylinder, which should be insulated, or by an instant water heater. To avoid further heat loss and scalds, the temperature should be set to 50°C or lower. Good insulation can save 250 carbs a year.

If you have a shower every day and your water is heated by gas, this will release 40 carbs a year. A full bath uses eight times as much water and a power shower may use five times as much.

When hot water is used for hand washing of dishes and clothes etc. don't leave the hot tap running but put the plug in the sink. Put more items in the machines. A household may thus save 30 litres of hot water each day and cut emissions by up to 100 carbs a year or 250 carbs if you have electric water heating.

– Lighting

Some household lights still use "incandescent" bulbs but "fluorescent" lights are now much more common and they are five times more efficient. Conventional fluorescent strip lights give a harsh, cold light but Compact Fluorescent Lights (CFLs) are warmer. They are the same size as old fashioned bulbs but use only 20% of the power. When all the remaining incandescent bulbs are replaced the UK will emit 8 million tonnes less CO_2. LEDs (light emitting diodes) are an alternative to CFLs. They are potentially more efficient and have a longer lifetime than CFLs but they are currently rather expensive. However, they appear to be developing into a viable and economic alternative.

– In the Kitchen

About a third of domestic electricity is consumed in the kitchen and there are a number of simple steps you can take to save electricity here:

- only boil as much water as you need
- boil water in an electric kettle not on the hob
- heat or cook small quantities of food in the microwave, larger quantities in the oven
- most modern electrical appliances are rated on a scale of A to G where A are the most efficient. In general B rated appliances uses 20% more electricity than A-rated ones while C-rated ones uses 40% more.

The average kitchen is responsible for about 500 carbs per person per year. Buying efficient appliances and using everything more carefully can cut this to 350 carbs. This may necessitate some capital outlay and there are also environmental consequences in replacing equipment before it is completely worn out.

– Laundry

An A-rated washer dryer uses almost 1 unit per load when washing but in drying mode it uses 3.4 units per load. Drying is an expensive process so use a washing line. Typically, a household of four will release 150 carbs per person washing clothes. With care this might be cut to about 100 carbs.

– Standby

On standby TV sets, DVD players or computers, perhaps surprisingly, still use some power. The total savings made in my household by turning items off at the wall rather than on the front of the item concerned are shown in the adjacent table. These figures very much depend on the actual models you have. It is quite likely that in the future redesign of equipment will eliminate the waste of electricity while equipment is on standby.

Carbs/yr from equipment left on standby	
TV Set	40
Digibox	65
DVD player	35
Three radios	60
PC	45
PC Screen	30
PC Speakers	30
Two Laptops	60
Router	10
Printer	60
Cooker	175
Total	**630**

– Overall Domestic Savings

The total number of carbs released as a result of domestic energy consumption in the UK is 2,400 per person per year. The table below gives an estimate of how much the average output of CO_2 could be reduced without any significant change in lifestyle – we just have to be more careful.

Domestic Energy Consumption – Carbs currently released per person and potential savings	Carbs	
	Now	Saving
Space Heating – efficient boiler, insulate walls and ceilings, fit double glazing, drop day time temperature to 18°C, night to 15°C, eliminate draughts, fit thermostatic radiator valves.	1,150	500
Hot water – insulate cylinder, store water at 50°C, use shower not bath, avoid power showers, minimise hand washing, turn off hot tap when not needed. An instant water heater could save another 100 carbs.	500	200
Lighting – use all energy efficient bulbs/turn lights off.	200	100
In the kitchen – buy A-rated appliances, use microwave where appropriate, don't boil more water than needed.	200	80
Laundry – don't do part loads, use tumble drier sparingly.	150	70
TV, computers etc. – leave nothing on standby.	200	150
Total per person per year	**2,400**	**1,100**

The Footprint From Travel

– Sixty Years of Change

Passenger travel and freight transport of one sort and another now account for 34% of our carbon footprint in the UK.

The distance we each travel within the UK has increased by a factor of almost four since 1955 as shown in the first chart on the next page and we now travel over 17,000 km each. Use of public buses and trains has fallen from 53% of the total to only 9% while air travel has increased from almost zero to 29% of the total.

The second chart on the next page shows that in 1955 the distance travelled by bus was the same as by car. We now go 14 km by car for every one km on a bus.

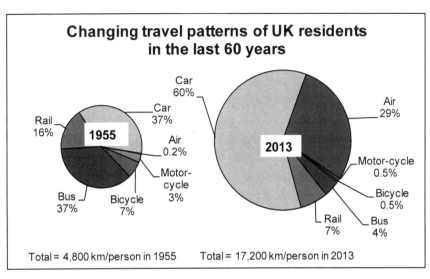

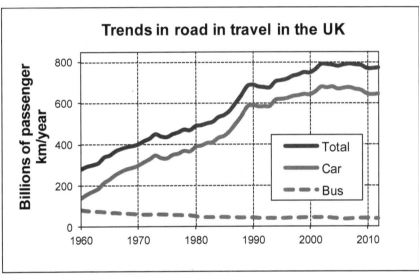

- Air Travel

The distance we fly has grown by a factor of six over the last thirty years to a total of 5,000 km each. Two thirds of our "air miles" are on holiday and almost a quarter while visiting friends and relations, really another form of holiday. Only 12% of our journeys are on business.

- Freight

In 1955 freight transport amounted to 1,900 tonne km per person. By 2012 this figure had risen to 4,300 tonne km per person. The proportion by road has increased from 40% to 64% largely at the expense of rail.

- Overall Contributions

As said earlier, transport accounts for 34% of our carbon footprint. The use of passenger cars clearly dominates but road freight and air traffic, mostly international passenger flights, also make a substantial contribution.

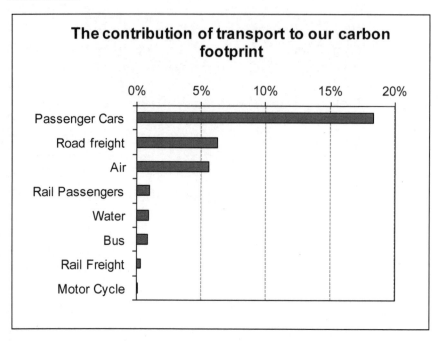

The contribution of transport to our carbon footprint

Passenger Transport

The steps we might take to reduce the impact of travel on the environment include the following:

- travelling less in total
- walking or using a bicycle when we can
- using public transport instead of a car
- travelling by road or rail instead of flying
- selecting a fuel efficient vehicle in the first place - a Lamborghini Roadster produces five time as much CO_2 as a VW Polo travelling the same distance
- drive any car we are using more economically. At 120 km/h (75 mph) we use 25% more fuel than when driving at 50-90 km/h (30-60 mph).

- Electric Cars

A typical electric car, such as a G-Wiz, is small. These cars have received considerable publicity some of which is misleading. One website claims that such a car has zero CO_2 emissions. Indeed no CO_2 is emitted from the exhaust but it is, at present, released in the UK during generation of most of the electricity used to charge the batteries. However, this would be less true in France, where much more nuclear power is used.

However, even in the UK an electric car is good for the environment, but mainly because it is likely to be small rather than because it is electric.

- Buses And Trains

In the UK buses and coaches have a surprisingly low load factor with only about nine passengers on board the average bus. Trains tend to have higher load factors. For most services it is about 30%, while for intercity services it is 40%. Electric trains put power back into the system when they are braking so CO_2 emissions are 50% less.

- Flying

There is a considerable amount of overseas air travel by UK residents as well as some within the UK. CO_2 released at high altitude has more impact on the climate because of the interaction of this CO_2 with other chemicals released at the same time and with ozone, water vapour and other chemicals already in the atmosphere. Many experts argue that for high altitude flights the amount of CO_2 emitted should be multiplied by a radiative forcing factor of about three.

- Comparison Of Modes

The most suitable unit for comparing the impact of different transport modes is grams of carbon dioxide per passenger kilometre (g CO_2/pkm) including that released when related electricity is generated.

The table on the next page shows the amount of CO_2 released by various forms of public transport assuming realistic load factors (i.e. numbers of passengers per vehicle) and by different cars. Buses and trains release less CO_2 per passenger than even the most efficient car going the same distance. However, with four people in a car you have to divide output by four when cars become more competitive. Aircraft are much less efficient but not as bad as cruise ships!

CO_2 from Public Transport and from Cars		
	grams per passenger km	
	In town	Out of Town
Bus/coach	90	30
London Underground	80	
Diesel train	90	70
Electric train	60	40
Average all passenger rail journeys	70	
Air - avg. inc. radiative forcing factor of 2.7	300	
Cruising at sea	850	
	grams CO_2 per vehicle km	
G-Wiz electric car charged in UK	84	
Most efficient petrol car (SEAT Ibiza)	140	80
Family saloon (Peugeot 307 Diesel)	220	130
Average Car (Peugeot 307 Petrol)	280	160
Gas Guzzler (Range Rover – 4.2 V8)	530	300
Most thirsty (Lamborghini 147 Roadster)	700	400

- What Could Be Achieved?

Most of our travel footprint comes from use of cars within the UK plus air travel. Here are some of the options for reducing CO_2 emissions using existing technology.

- Use public transport more and share cars more so as to increase load factors.

- Choose a smaller car. The average UK car today uses 8.8 l of fuel per 100 km and releases 280 g CO_2/km while the most efficient vehicle available uses half this amount of fuel and releases only 140 g CO_2/km.

- Drive economically. Most drivers could probably reduce their consumption by 10% by driving more carefully.

- One option is to give up owning a car altogether. If you don't actually own a car you will use public transport most of the time.

- Fly less - most air travel is a luxury. On a return flight to Malaga we each release a tonne of CO_2. The same distance on an electric train will release only 135 kg CO_2 based on UK power generation.

- Walk and cycle more.

The steps above are relatively easy to implement and require little change in lifestyle. To be effective it will require a change of attitude and an adjustment of priorities. Perhaps we need to use pricing policies as further encouragement.

Here are two scenarios for reducing our travel footprint: The first is a realistic scenario based on changes we could easily make to our travel. The optimistic scenario would require more effort and perhaps involve some inconvenience.

Alternative Scenarios for Reducing our Travel Footprint	
Realistic	**Optimistic**
Halve air travel and do the rest by train	Divide air travel by three and do the rest by train
Treble the distance travelled by bus and train	Quadruple the distance travelled by bus and train
Walk or cycle four times more	Walk or cycle four times more
Reduce remaining amount of land travel by 10% and only use a car for these journeys	Reduce remaining amount of land travel by 20% and only use a car for these journeys
Choose to use public transport and share cars more to increase load factors as follows: - cars and trains 30% to 40% - local bus & tube 20% to 30% - rail 30% to 40% - air travel 70% to 80%	Choose to use public transport and share cars more to increase load factors as follows: - cars and trains 30% to 50% - local bus and tube 20% to 40% - rail 30% to 50% - air travel 70% to 80%
Reduce consumption of cars from 8.8 l/100 km to 6.1 l/100 km - half way between the current average and that of the most economical vehicle available. Achieved by selecting smaller cars and driving more economically. Does not include additional use of small electric cars.	Reduce fuel consumption of cars from 8.8 l/100 km to 5.0 l/100 km – 75% of the way from the current average and that of the most economical vehicles. Achieved by selecting even smaller cars and continuing to drive economically. Even more saving could be achieved if small electric cars were widely used.

The Realistic Scenario only involves modest changes in behaviour and a drop of about 10% in the total distance travelled. The biggest problem will be to persuade people to switch from air to rail for some of their foreign travel. The Optimistic Scenario takes all these changes a little further and requires some of the overseas travel to be abandoned.

The impact of these scenarios on the distance we travel is shown in the next chart. There is a switch from car and air travel to bus and rail but only a small overall change in the total distance travelled. The impact on CO_2 emissions, however, is dramatic. The Realistic Scenario reduces the carbs resulting from our travel by 50% or our total carbs by 14%. For the Optimistic Scenario the corresponding figures are 64% and 18%.

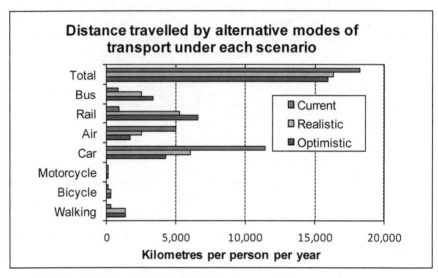

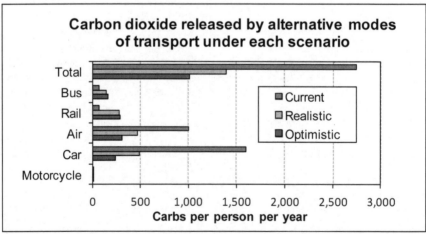

These calculations involve all sorts of assumptions and approximations. Although experts might quarrel about the details, the overall conclusion is robust – we really can substantially reduce our travel footprint. If we won't do this voluntarily then laws or financial incentives must make us do it.

- Freight Transport

The movement of freight within the UK has gone up by a factor of two and a half in the last fifty years and is now at 4,300 tonne km per person. Freight now accounts for about 7% of our overall carbon footprint. Although the total freight moved has risen by a factor of two and a half, the volume moved by road has increased four and a half times.

The increase in freight movements is partly because there are more of us but mostly because we each consume more things and source less of our products locally. Industry has become globalised and the distance between factory and customer has increased dramatically. We are no longer content to eat food only when it is in season in UK and this necessitates delivery from distant overseas sources.

On average rail freight puts about 30 g of CO_2 into the atmosphere for every tonne km of goods transported. The corresponding figure for road freight is an average of 170 g. However, railways go from point to point rather than door to door and we still need local road transport for collection and final delivery. Furthermore, the road figure is an average and depends on the size of the truck and the load factor. Smaller goods vehicles, with load factors of perhaps 25% and the higher urban fuel consumption emit 750 g of CO_2 per tonne km while larger articulated trucks with a load factor of 50% emit only 100 grams. If these trucks could be operated with higher load factors then their emissions could be comparable with those from rail transport.

CO₂ emissions and freight transport	
Mode of transport	**g CO₂/ tonne km**
Road	
Light goods in town	750
Heavy goods out of town	100
Rail	30
Sea	
Small Ro-Ro	60
Large Ro-Ro	20
Small bulk cargo	14
Large bulk cargo	7
Air (inc. radiative forcing)	
Short haul	3,000
Long haul	1,500

Figures on CO_2 emissions for goods transported by air and sea are also summarised in the table above together with the figures for road and rail transport. On land, rail would clearly be the most attractive if it were not for the need, generally, to collect and deliver by road at each end of the journey. At sea, there is a big difference between small ships and bulk cargo - the latter is easily the least polluting form of freight transport. The most striking feature of the table is the high level of emissions from airfreight.

We, as individuals, have significant control over the carbon footprint which arises from our choices concerning our own travel but very much less about the impact of freight. We cannot directly reverse globalisation but we can, to some extent choose products which are sourced locally. Even where we can make choices it is not necessarily clear what the impact will be. It has been estimated that less energy is used to truck tomatoes from Spain to UK than would be used to grow them at home, out of season in a heated greenhouse. We should really only eat them in season!

The travel history of some products is clearly absurd but supermarkets do not, in general, go out of their way to waste money. There may be savings of money and/or energy by bulk handling and storage, particularly where products need chilling or freezing.

To provide a context for the savings we might consider, here are a few examples where we may have some choice about what to buy:

- Really local fruit or vegetables may have travelled less than 50 km. If you buy 10 kg a week from local sources then in a year its transport will have generated about 4 carbs. If it had travelled a typical route via distribution centres then it might have generated 40 carbs.

- Wine is often, though not always, bottled where it is made. A case coming from the South of France by rail would release 0.5 carbs. Coming from Australia in a large bulk carrier would release 1.8 carbs. If you drink a case a month of Australian rather than French wine then transport will add 16 carbs (0.16%) to your carbon footprint - the equivalent of driving just over 100 km in your car.

- Strawberries are often flown in from Kenya when home grown ones are out of season and their journey releases 10 carbs per kg. A kilo a month would add about 1% to your footprint if they are flown on a dedicated cargo flight although if they were in part of the hold of a passenger plane which would otherwise have been empty then the figure could be a quarter of this. If we choose not to buy them, then we do reduce emissions but what impact do we have on the lives of poor Kenyan farmers for whom strawberries may be a major source of income. But would they then grow the food their urban compatriots need so badly?

- Strawberries have to be flown in because they do not keep long. Apples, oranges and bananas keep much longer and can be transported by sea. Fruit from South Africa or the Caribbean coming by sea releases less than 0.1 carbs per kilogram so, even if you eat 1 kg a week, transport for a year's supply is only equivalent to that for a single half kg of strawberries flown in from Kenya.

Freight contributes about 7% to our carbon footprint but there are a few choices we can make as individuals to influence this. One thing we can realistically do is to try to buy local products but remembering that there may be other factors which offset the savings we think we have made. The second step is to avoid buying products which have been flown into the country.

Conclusions are not straight forward but a saving of 20% would not be unreasonable if industry takes steps to increase load factors and we all choose to buy locally made products when we can. This would reduce our overall footprint by about 1.5%.

Industry

In the UK, almost 40% of our carbon footprint comes from the use of energy in the manufacturing and services sectors and achieving reductions here is complicated. It is not always a straightforward process to decide the best solution as a number of factors may interact. Although we may be able to see an opportunity for reduction of emissions, our personal decisions usually have little direct impact. This, however, does not prevent us from lobbying politicians and decision makers or deliberately selecting products which appear to have less environmental impact.

A quarter of our carbon footprint in the UK comes from industrial production, including agriculture. The chart on the next page shows the contribution of different sectors. The figures relate only to production in the UK itself. There is also CO_2 produced in the manufacture of goods produced overseas which we import and this adds to our real footprint. This, in part, is offset by the fact that a small part of the goods produced in the UK are exported and the CO_2 released in their production should be seen as part of someone else's footprint rather than part of ours.

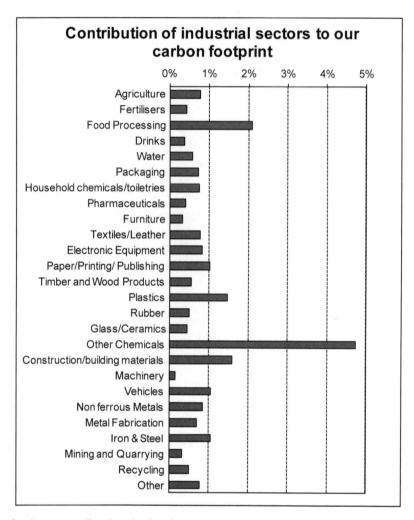

A further complication is the fact that there is no double counting in the calculations. Thus the CO_2 released in production of fertilisers is not included in that resulting from agriculture so that the total emission from production of food raw materials is the sum of that from both these sectors. In this case the calculation is easy since all the fertiliser goes to agriculture.

However, the total energy involved in production of vehicles also includes some of that involved in making iron and steel or non-ferrous metals. The chart tells us what proportion of energy goes directly to vehicle production but does not tell us what we should add for the component metals. However, although the chart is neither 100% accurate nor 100% complete it certainly highlights a number of features which are worthy of consideration. I do not propose to go into a detailed analysis of each sector but here are some examples of the complexity involved in determining the footprint of particular types of products as well as some other points of interest:

- The first four activities, agriculture, fertilisers, food processing and drinks are almost exclusively involved in production of food. It is interesting to see that food-processing accounts for 2% of our footprint and this does not include cooking at home. In addition water, packaging, transport, retail services, warehousing and hotels and catering are also involved. Determining the footprint associated with food is particularly complex.

- The energy involved in construction and building materials covers most of that involved in building but there are other elements. Part of the freight transport is involved with building materials. Mining and quarrying also contribute, as do part of plastics and glass and some of timber and wood products.

- From the chart, vehicle manufacturing accounts for 1% of our total footprint but the complete sum for vehicles would also include parts of machinery, non-ferrous metals, iron & steel and metal fabrication, as mentioned earlier, as well as plastics and rubber.

This cursory look at the manufacturing sector is all we need at this stage since our personal decisions have little direct influence. However, manufacturing accounts for 24% of our total footprint so there is potential for a significant reduction. Furthermore, if we waste less products and recycle more, a long-term saving of 20% in our footprint related to manufacturing would not be unreasonable.

Services

The chart on the next page shows how the 14% share of our carbon footprint that comes from the services sector is divided between different activities. A great deal of the energy is concerned with heating using mainly gas, as well as air conditioning and lighting, both of which rely on electricity.

Almost 4% of our footprint is associated with retailing and another 2% with hotels and catering. The figure for retailing is about the same as the total from government, education, health and commercial offices.

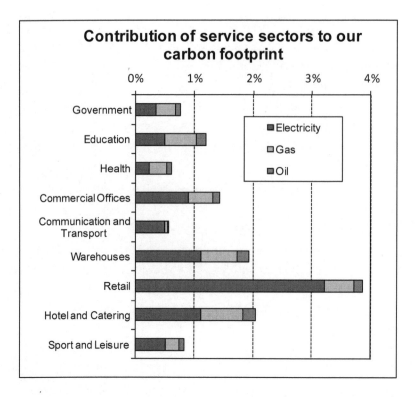

As with the manufacturing sector, there is little we can do through our personal decisions to influence these figures except for lobbying government and commercial organisations. The public sector is already reasonably good with lighting and most street lighting has for years used what we would now call low energy bulbs. Light sensitive switches are increasingly in use to turn them on as needed between dusk and dawn. Some people are concerned that this introduces a security risk.

Commercial organisations are beginning to make "green noises" and many of the large retailers make "green" offers where they interface directly with their customers but it is difficult to tell if this is just window dressing or if real changes are being made. We frequently see incentives to recycle plastic bags or to use less of them but the impact of this on our overall

---

Comparing Bags

Most supermarkets offer biodegradable plastic bags If I use one of these a day this will add about 0.06% to my carbon footprint over a year. If I use a reusable "bag for life" and use it 30 times this will have a similar impact on my footprint. The impact of a paper carrier bag is 20 times that of a biodegradable bag. If I use a cotton or jute bag I will need to reuse it 400 times for it to compete with the biodegradable plastic bag.

footprint is very small as described in the box above. What organisations have to do is make real changes even when the changes are hidden from the public gaze.

The service sector accounts for 14% of our footprint and again it would not be unreasonable to expect a 20% long-term reduction in this figure simply by increasing efficiency and avoiding waste. This would reduce our overall footprint by about 3%.

Overall Savings

In this Chapter I have given an overview of the contribution to our footprint of some of our activities in the UK. I have identified choices we could make which, if we all adopted them, could reduce the national footprint significantly. In other areas I have made a guess of possible savings. The next table summarises the potential reductions of our footprint identified in this chapter. The reduction could be about a third of the current total footprint.

Many people now recognise that Climate Change is a problem and that we need to do something about it. However, most of the time we do very little to help if it puts us to any inconvenience or any expense. We can all lobby government and commercial organisations to make changes which will reduce energy consumption but in the end it is **down to us**.

Potential Reductions in our Carbon Footprint			
Sector	Current per Capita Footprint (Carbs)	Potential Savings	
		Carbs	Percent
Domestic	2,400	900	36%
Travel	2,400	1,200	50%
Freight	500	100	20%
Manufacturing	2,000	400	20%
Services	1,200	240	20%
	8,500	2,840	33%

We can do all this now without the introduction of renewable energy and it would of course help us to reduce CO_2 emissions now. It is important to adopt these changes in our behaviour as they will not only reduce CO_2 in the short-term but will, perhaps more importantly, reduce the quantity of renewables which we will need in the future.

Chapter 7

The Population Explosion

Heading For Disaster

If man has been responsible for the recent changes in the climate then, if we want to consider how the climate will change in the future we need to look at how the World population is likely to continue growing.

By 10,000 BC the worldwide population of Homo Sapiens was about four million. Today there are seventy-three cities with more people than this. Over the 10,000 years up to the birth of Christ the population grew steadily until it had reached around 200 million – more than doubling every 2,000 years.

It took another 1,400 years for the population to double again. Then the pace began to increase and it doubled again reaching 750 million by about 1760. The pace continued to accelerate and in 1900, after another 140 years, the population had reached 1.5 billion. Between 1900 and 1960 it increased to 3 billion before reaching 6 billion at the start of the current millennium. It is now at about 7.2 billion. The chart illustrates these changes with the population doubling in each of the five bands.

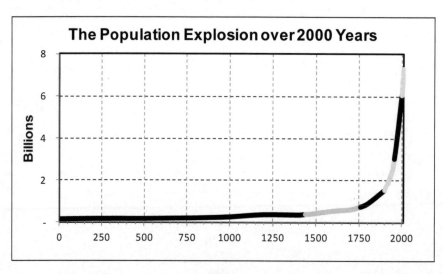

If the whole of man's existence is represented by twenty-four hours then the World population has doubled in the last seven seconds and quadrupled in the last seventeen! The term **"population explosion"** *doesn't look like an exaggeration.*

A Ray Of Hope

The next chart shows how the population growth rate has changed since the year 1000 – the growth rate is the percentage change from one year to the next. Up to 1700 the rate was modest but from then on it began to increase, slowly at first but then much more rapidly from 1900, largely as a result of the reduction in child mortality. It reached a peak of 2% per year in 1970.

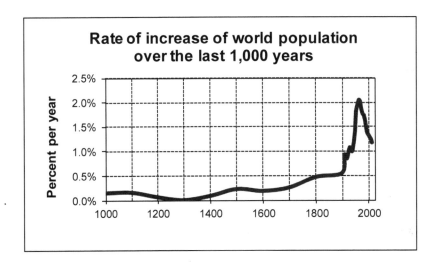

Alarming though population growth in the last century may look, there is one encouraging sign. Since 1970 the worldwide growth rate has shown a steady decrease and this has continued into the new millennium. But remember a decline in the rate of growth does not mean the population is going down but only that it is growing less quickly than before but **there is no room for complacency**. If the current growth rate of about 1.2% continues then, at the turn of the next century, my great grandchildren will be sharing the planet with about 20 billion other people – almost three times as many of us as there are today.

Regional Differences

The total World population grew more than two and a half times between 1950 and 2014 but there were big regional differences. The table below shows that in Africa there are now five times as many people as in 1950. Even in Europe the population has gone up by a over a third.

Population Changes 1950 to 2014				
Region	Millions		Ratio 2014/ 1950	Compound annual inc.
	1950	2014		
Europe & Russia	547	741	1.4	0.5%
North America	172	365	2.1	1.2%
China	555	1,365	2.5	1.4%
Oceania	13	38	3.5	1.7%
India	358	1,245	3.4	2.0%
Asia	490	1,688	3.5	2.0%
Latin America	167	615	3.7	2.1%
Africa	221	1,111	5.0	2.6%
World Total	2,523	7,168	2.8	1.6%

The chart below shows the proportion of the population in each of the eight regions in 2014. Asia, when India and China are included, accounts for 60% of the current total. Just ten of the World's roughly 200 countries account for 60% of the total population. Three of these, Pakistan, Bangladesh and Nigeria, with current growth rates over 2% are a cause of particular concern.

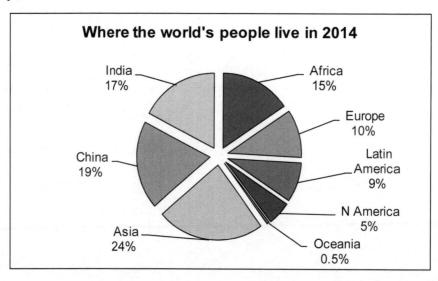

Where the world's people live in 2014

India 17%
Africa 15%
Europe 10%
Latin America 9%
N America 5%
Oceania 0.5%
Asia 24%
China 19%

Population Growth Rates

In Mediaeval Europe life expectancy at birth was about twenty-seven. Since then it has increased to over 80 in the Developed World. In the past mothers had large numbers of children but many of them died in childhood. As child mortality dropped, more children survived to have children of their own and populations escalated dramatically in only a generation or two. It was this drop in child mortality, without any access to birth control, combined with greater overall life expectancy that led to the population explosion in the eighteen and nineteen hundreds.

The drop in child mortality happens very rapidly as modern medicine moves into a community and it takes two or three generations for people to believe this is permanent so initially they go on having just as many children as before and populations increase dramatically. Once people believe this drop in child mortality is permanent they often take steps to have less children and then the growth rate falls although this drop will be significantly influenced by cultural and religious factors.

The next chart illustrates how population growth rates have changed, region by region, over the last sixty years. Africa gives the most cause for concern but even here the growth rate is lower now than it was in 1950 and well below the peak in 1980. Overall the worldwide growth rate has almost halved in the last fifty years.

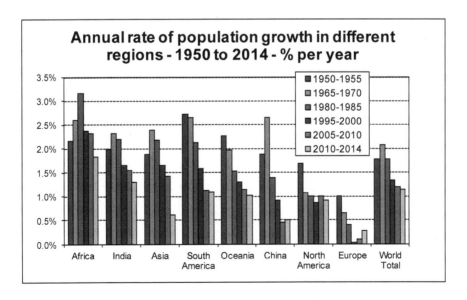

Once life expectancy levels off the crucial factor is the number of children a woman has, i.e. her total fertility rate (TFR). When this drops to two then the population will eventually stabilise. The chart below shows how fertility rates have changed over the last 50 years in a selection of countries. Saudi Arabia started with a very high rate but this has dropped dramatically. Least Developed Countries (LDCs) have shown a similar drop since 1950 but China is the best example of how a concerted effort can yield results.

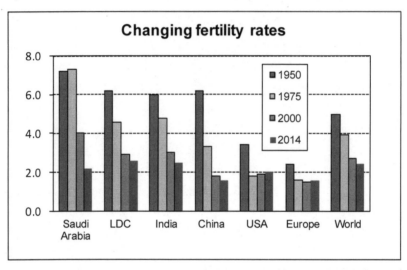

There are many reasons to expect that the decline in fertility rates will continue. According to a UN fertility report both men and women in Developing Countries were marrying two years later in the 1990s than in the 1970s. In Developed Countries the delay was over three years. Over the same period the use of modern contraception by married women increased from 27% to 40% in Developing Countries. In 1976 over half of all countries had no active government involvement in family planning. By 2001, 92% of governments supported family planning programmes and the distribution of contraceptives and it is essential that this continues.

Trends such as these are moving in the right direction and the overall World fertility has fallen from 5.0 in 1950 down to 2.4 in 2014. In 2000 there were still 76 countries with fertility rates of over 3 - between them these accounted for almost 20% of the World population. By 2014 the number of countries with fertility rates over 3 had fallen to 53 and they now account for 15% of the world population. Between them these countries have an average TFR of 4.7.

The table below lists the 29 of these countries which also have populations above 10 million. It is clear from the table where the biggest problems lie, but reducing fertility is not an impossible task. As well as providing family planning advice and contraceptives, many countries will need to concentrate on education to counter the cultural tradition of large families as well as dealing with religious taboos.

Countries With A Population Over 10 Million And A Total Fertility Rate (TFR) Over 3.0 In 2014								
	Pop (M)	TFR		Pop (M)	TFR		Pop (M)	TFR
Niger	17	6.9	Mozambique	25	5.4	Madagascar	21	4.3
Mali	16	6.2	Nigeria	179	5.3	Yemen	26	4.1
Somalia	11	6.1	Ethiopia	88	5.2	Ghana	27	4.1
Uganda	35	6.0	Tanzania	45	5.0	Sudan	37	3.9
Burkina Faso	17	5.9	Guinea	11	4.9	Ivory Coast	23	3.6
Zambia	15	5.8	Cameroon	20	4.8	Zimbabwe	13	3.6
Malawi	16	5.7	D Rep C	69	4.8	Kenya	42	3.5
Afghanistan	26	5.4	Chad	13	4.7	Iraq	36	3.4
Angola	20	5.4	Rwanda	11	4.6	Philippines	100	3.1
South Sudan	11	5.4	Senegal	14	4.5	TOTAL	983	4.7

The Future Population

Will the explosion continue? The chart below shows the actual growth in World population from 1950 to 2014 with UN projections to 2150. When making these projections the most difficult task is predicting fertility rates. The three projections are each based on different estimates of likely fertility. Figures beyond 2050 are very uncertain.

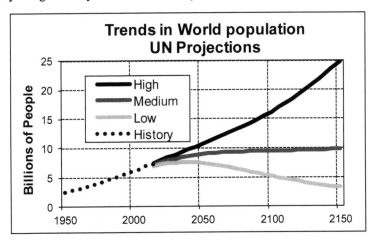

73

The medium forecast is the most likely and suggests that the World population will level off at about 10 billion. This would be a substantial increase on the present figure but is well below the catastrophic levels that have sometimes been predicted.

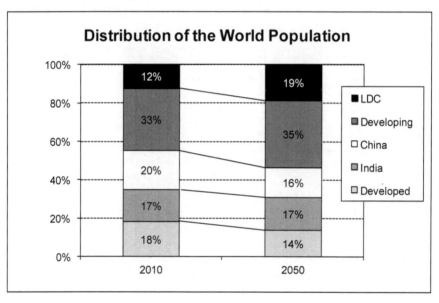

Different countries will grow at different rates and the differences will continue well into the future so the relative importance of regions will change as shown in the chart above. The Least Developed Countries, whose populations are increasing fastest, will account for an increasing share of the World population. The chart illustrates the changes between 2010 and 2050 based on the medium growth forecast. The change in the proportions in different regions will almost certainly lead to some shift in the political balance between regions.

The 10 billion forecast of population was originally presented by the UN as the most likely level by the end of the century. They have recently qualified their view and suggest that the population could go up as high as 15 billion. This estimate was only presented by them as a possibility rather than a probability and it could serve as an alarm bell which will lead to positive steps to reduce birth rates in particular countries.

What We Must Do

How the population grows is critical to the survival of the Human race. It will directly affect our use of all resources in general and the burning of fossil fuels in particular as well as longer term demand for renewable energy. This in turn will determine our impact on the climate. It is essential to keep numbers down to a manageable level. It looks as if the total population may level off at about 10 billion although it could be significantly higher. In the long run there may be a decline. It is also worth noting that we should avoid steps which might lead to a rapid decline. This would lead to an increasing proportion of elderly people with declining numbers of young people to support them in their old age.

Since most of us would agree that interfering with the increasing trend in life expectancy is unacceptable, we will have to keep up the efforts to reduce fertility in those countries where the TFR is currently well above two. This will require continuing education to counter cultural attitudes and ignorance about birth control. As we have seen above the trends are in the right direction.

The immediate question is "Can the World support a likely population of 10 billion?". In subsequent chapters we will look at how a population of this size can be supplied with sufficient energy and how this may affect the climate. Clearly a population of 15 billion would be significantly more difficult to sustain.

Chapter 8

Where Are We Going?

The Starting Point

So far we have been looking at how we, the World, arrived where we are with the environment and climate we have today. Now we want to look at where energy consumption may go in the future.

Man's impact on the climate arises primarily from the burning of fossil fuels which increases the level of greenhouse gases in the atmosphere. The rate of increase in the GHGs will depend on how much each of us produce, how many of us there are in the World, as discussed in the previous chapter, and how long a particular gas remains in the atmosphere. To forecast future Climate Change we need to look both at changing patterns of energy usage and at population growth but it is important to recognise at the outset that forecasting is not an exact science.

Predictions From Past Trends

Perhaps the simplest way of forecasting the future is to look at how things have changed in the past and to assume that the pattern of change will continue into the future. But we have to be careful.

The chart illustrates how an erroneous prediction might be made. The solid line shows how the average height of boys increases with age, reaching a steady value of about 178 cm (5ft 10in) at the age of 20. If I only had data for the early years I

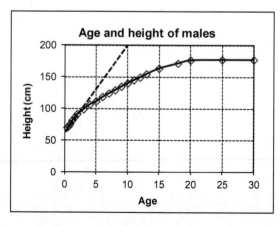

might assume that the same rate of growth over the initial three year period would continue and that before the age of 10 my three year old grandson would be a 2 metre (6ft 7in) giant as shown by the dashed line. We have to be very careful how we interpret trends.

Trends In CO_2 Levels

Chapter 3 showed the long-term historical change in the concentration of CO_2 in the atmosphere. The chart below shows how the average annual CO_2 levels, as measured at the Mauna Loa Observatory in Hawaii, have risen from about 350 ppm (parts per million) in 1990 to almost 400 ppm in 2013. The CO_2 levels vary annually with a peak in April about 7 ppm higher than the minimum in October. This cycle is the result of absorption of CO_2 by plants growing during the summer months in the Northern hemisphere. As a result of this cycle, in April 2014, levels of CO_2 reached 400 ppm for the first time in the last million years, although the average for the year is a little less than this.

From this chart it looks as though there has been a steady increase of around 2 ppm per year. If this increase continues then by 2050 the CO_2 level will have risen to over 470 ppm .

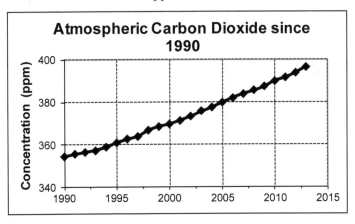

The chart on the next page, based on exactly the same figures as the previous one, shows the amount by which CO_2 has increased year by year since 1990. There are fluctuations in the rate of increase from year to year partly as a result of seasonal variations in weather which affect the growth of vegetation in different places. The figures are erratic but there has been some increase every year. The data allows for two very different interpretation.

From the earlier chart the average increase is about 2 ppm per year. From this chart there is an overall upward, though erratic, trend in the rate of increase of CO_2 in the atmosphere.

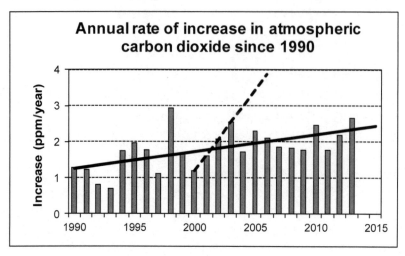

The solid line suggest that this rate has accelerated from 1.2 ppm per year in 1990 to 2.4 ppm by 2013. If this pattern continues then the rate of increase will have more than doubled by 2050. On this basis the level of CO_2 will have reached over 500 ppm by the middle of this century.

Early in 2004 concern was expressed that the rate of increase appeared to be accelerating since the trend for the years 2000 to 2003, shown by the dashed line, indicated a much higher rate of increase. If this trend were to continue then, by 2050, CO_2 would be over 800 ppm. When results for 2004 became available it appeared that this concern was unfounded.

The question remains, "how fast will CO_2 levels grow in the future?" In the previous paragraphs we have made three significantly different predictions. These predictions are illustrated in the first chart on the next page. The "Linear" line shows historical figures up to 2013 and then assumes that levels continue to increase at a steady rate of 1.9 ppm per year which is the average annual increase from 1990 to 2013. The "Likely" line assumes that the increase accelerates steadily as calculated from the solid line in the previous chart. The "Extreme" line is based just on data for the years 2000 to 2003.

These figures illustrate the problems which frequently arise when making forecasts. Usually the best approach is to use all the data you have but to remain alive to the possibility that you may be wrong. On the basis of the trends in the recent figures it appears that atmospheric CO_2 is likely to reach about 800 ppm by 2100 unless something is done to modify the trend.

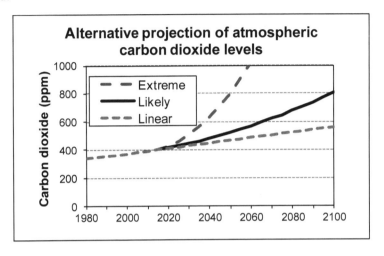

Global Temperature Trends

In Chapter 3 we looked at the change in the Earth's surface temperature over the last half million years or so and also at more recent changes. The grey line in the chart below shows how the average temperature has increased each year since 1900. The figures from year to year are somewhat erratic, partly as a result of uncertainty in the measurements, but partly also as a result of variations in the atmosphere which can arise from local weather changes or events such as earthquakes or volcanoes.

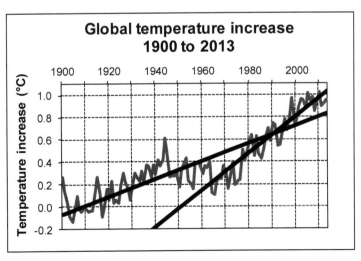

There is little doubt that there is an overall upward trend. It seems clear there was an increase from 1900 to 1945 followed by dimming until 1970 and then the more rapid rise to the present day. The solid line shows the average trend over the whole period with a rise of a little over 0.6°C in the last century. The dashed line, however, shows the trend over the last thirty years. If the latter trend continues then the temperature will rise by a further 2°C in this century. As usual when you make predictions from trends the result depends on how you select the data but a further 2°C by 2100 is clearly a possibility and we need to consider how we can mitigate the impact.

Predictions From Models

Apart from looking at trends, more sophisticated forecasts can be made by building models but this again is not a precise science and always involves making assumptions and approximations. If you have an understanding of a process and can write an equation for how various variables interact then you have the basis for a model.

The mathematical models that economists and scientists frequently use to make predictions arrive at more robust conclusions than just working with trends. However, the trends themselves do help in determining the assumptions it is appropriate to build into the model. But remember, the experts by no means always agree on what assumptions should be made and we often end up with a variety of predictions depending on the assumptions that have been made.

- Models Of The Climate

Real models may have many variables which interact with each other. Making forecasts can be extremely complex and this is certainly true for the Climate. We need to make assumptions about how many people there will be and then how much energy we will each use. We need to make assumptions about fertility and mortality rates, region by region, so that we can forecast the overall population growth. We need to make assumptions about economic progress so that we can estimate energy consumption and the use of fossil fuels.

Now we can begin to build a model for the climate. The atmosphere and the oceans have to be divided into many separate elements. We have to look at how these elements interact with each other and with the oceans.

As the air heats up, the sea also gets warmer. CO_2 dissolves less quickly and so its concentration in the atmosphere builds up faster and the air gets hotter so the sea gets even warmer ... . Then of course a major change in climate could affect the size of the World's population which would affect energy consumption and then CO_2 emissions ... . All this takes us back to where we started two paragraphs earlier and round the loop we go again. We may have to go many, many times round the loop before we arrive at consistent solutions.

- Modelling The Past

The rest of this chapter is based on data from IPCC (Intergovernmental Panel on Climate Change). They have created a climate model taking into account the factors discussed above together with many others both natural and anthropogenic.

The first test of any model is to see how well it reproduces observations from the past. In Chapter 3 we saw charts which showed how the change in the measured global temperature anomaly matched the values calculated with the IPCC model.

The fit between observations and calculated values helps to give confidence in the model. If a model were unable to "predict" the past then we would have difficulty in believing its predictions for the future. However, the fact that a model does predict the past does not "prove" that predictions for the future will be accurate.

Modelling The Future

The IPCC model referred to above, although tested by modelling the past, was designed to predict the future. Before it can be used for this, assumptions have to be made about how the World population and economy will develop in the future. In particular assumptions have to be made about the energy-related policies and practices which will be adopted by governments, commercial organisations and individuals. This is necessary so that we can arrive at values for the anthropogenic elements which have to be fed into the model.

World development over the next century could follow any number of paths and below are a set of storylines. These are based on two pairs of opposing ideas. We may continue along the **Materialistic (Mat)** route with ever-increasing consumption of resources or we may follow an **Alternative (Alt)** path more concerned with services and efficient use of resources. Secondly the World may continue to have wide differences in standards of living within and between countries, i.e. we remain **Fragmented (Frag).** On the other hand economies may become more **Convergent (Con)** with all the people throughout the World tending towards a more equal share of wealth.

If you are at all idealistic you would probably opt for one of the Alternative scenarios and of the other two choices I would go for the convergent one. Although this may lead to some loss of cultural diversity it should end up with a fairer distribution of wealth.

Predictions by IPCC of CO_2 levels over the next hundred years, based on different sets of assumptions, are shown in the chart below. If the World remains on its current material intensive, fossil-fuelled **(Fos)** course CO_2 emissions will increase by a factor of four by 2100. If the World adopts alternative technologies and renewables **(Ren)** then emissions could begin to decline by the middle of the century. Perhaps the most likely scenario involves continued convergence and materialism with a mix of renewable and fossil fuels **(MatCon+Mix).** This still leads to CO_2 emission levels at the end of the century almost double the current level. If we gradually move along this line, we shall begin to run out of fossil fuel and this will force us to look for alternatives. This, in turn, will drive us towards the AltCon or MatCon+Ren options shown by the lower two lines.

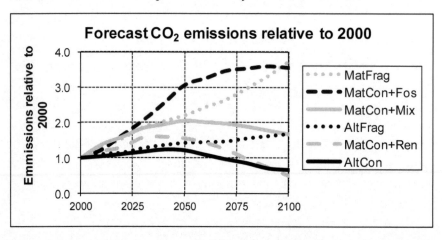

Forecast CO_2 emissions relative to 2000

The next chart shows that, whichever of these options dominates, the level of CO_2 will be up by at least 50% by 2100 but in the worst case it will be two and a half times higher than the present level.

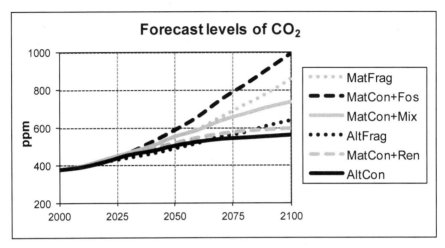

On page 79 we extrapolated the recent trend in the CO_2 levels and concluded it was "likely" to increase to 800 ppm by 2100. This much more sophisticated IPCC forecast arrives at a very similar figure unless there is a switch towards renewable fuels. It is always encouraging to arrive at similar conclusions via different routes.

The next chart shows how temperature will change. In the worst case it rises by a further 4°C above the level in 2000 while the most optimistic scenario predicts an increase of 2°C. In the light of the changes already recorded, even this looks like a cause for concern. We have to

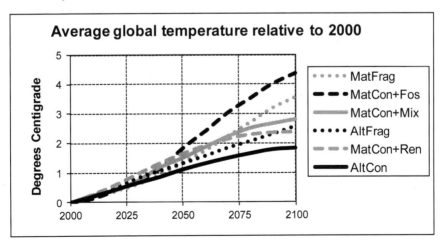

concentrate on looking for renewable sources of energy. Even the most optimistic prediction suggests the temperature will rise at 4 times the average rate for the last century and many times above the highest rate in the last 10,000 years.

Despite an increase in the average global temperature, rain and snow are likely to increase over most land areas, particularly polar regions and the mid Northern latitudes. Nearer the equator there will be some areas where rainfall decreases. The increase in average temperature may accentuate the effects of El Niño, as described in Chapter 2, and will result in wider year-to-year variations in rainfall and the summer monsoons of Asia. Potentially floods and drought will become more common.

In the Northern hemisphere sea-ice and glaciers will continue to retreat as is already happening in Greenland although the Antarctic ice sheet will increase in mass.

The IPCC scenarios lead to a rise in sea level of between 30 and 50 cm though the most extreme of their estimates suggest a rise of almost a metre. This may not sound very much but along the East Coast of the USA, for example, there are almost 60,000 km^2 of land only 1.5 m above sea-level. This is equivalent to a strip of land about 10km wide all along the coast from New England to Florida.

A Solution?

There are sceptics who deny that there is any man-made change and catastrophists who suggest the changes will be very much worse than suggested above.

If we take the "Sceptic" view and do nothing about Climate Change then, if we are wrong, the World may become a seriously less pleasant place in which to live. On the other hand we can assume that Climate Change is a reality and act accordingly. The downside of this is that it may cost money which might have been better spent elsewhere. In my view, it is almost certainly better to hedge our bets and accelerate our development of renewable energy, particularly as we will have to do so in the long run before we run out of fossil fuels.

On the other side of the argument are those who suggest that Climate Change has been seriously underestimated by IPCC. These views perhaps deserve to be considered more seriously. A tipping point can be reached where positive feedback can make things happen faster than expected. For example ice at the poles reflects some of the incident sunlight. If the Earth warms up and the ice melts then less sunlight is reflected and more is absorbed and hence the Earth heats up faster and faster as more and more ice melts so that more and more light is absorbed and so on ....

So what do we do? I think we have to accept that Climate Change is happening. We will have to learn to live with it while taking steps to keep it within bounds, as discussed in Chapters 11 and 12. In particular we need to replace fossil fuels with renewable energy but then we shall have to do this in the longer term anyway as fossil fuels will eventually run out. We need to remain watchful and modify our actions if it becomes apparent that the changes are more serious than we expected.

So far there has been lots of talk but little action. The Kyoto Protocol, which is discussed in more detail in Chapter 11, was signed by about 80 countries in 1997 but it only came into effect in 2005 when it was eventually ratified by Russia. The Protocol has never been ratified by the USA, one of the largest producers of GHGs. Under the Protocol the industrialised countries agreed that, by 2012, they would have reduced their emission of GHGs by 8%, compared to the 1990 levels.

Although Kyoto was a step in the right direction it has had only a very small impact on worldwide GHG emissions, which rose by 36% between 1990 and 2013. If it had not been for Kyoto, they might, perhaps, have risen by 40%, not a big difference. The time it has taken to set up this agreement illustrates the difficulty of getting international cooperation in areas such as this where costs are incurred now while benefits only arise in the more distant future.

There is a great deal more that still needs to be done. Fossil fuels cannot last forever so, irrespective of their adverse effect on the climate, we need to begin developing alternatives. We need to take action now and keep watching and questioning so that if the changes are faster than predicted we recognise it in time to take even more serious action.

Solutions are available but one country cannot solve the problem alone and getting the necessary agreement, let alone action, will not be easy. As discussed later global cooperation will be essential and although some efforts have been made in this direction the conclusions of the Copenhagen, Cancun, Durban and Doha conferences do not go nearly far enough in their efforts to reach a solution. Similarly, the Earth Summit in Rio in 2012 failed to set any concrete targets for countries to agree on with respect to the use of fossil fuels and reduction in emissions. Similarly, the conference in Warsaw in 2013, still failed to produce concrete results. In September 2014 a UN Climate Change Summit was held in New York attended by leaders of over 100 countries. Leaders of America and China both made positive statements with regard to cutting their emissions of GHGs but two days is hardly enough to reach any final agreement.

The 2014 Lima conferences has drafted targets to be finalised in Paris in December 2015. Will the necessary targets be agreed and, more importantly, will the necessary steps be taken to ensure that they are met?

An alternative solution sometimes suggested for limiting global warming is the use of geo-engineering. This involves large scale changes to the Earth's surface or atmosphere so that more energy is reflected back into space. This could involve covering deserts with reflective materials or putting dust particles or even very small reflectors into the upper atmosphere. There is no guarantee that these schemes would work and maintenance is likely to be a problem. There may also be unexpected consequences from tampering with the upper atmosphere. Geo-engineering is potentially dangerous and is not usually considered to be a serious option but it should not be entirely sidelined.

Chapter 9

The Energy We Will Need

My aim in this chapter is to arrive at an estimate of the total amount of energy the World will need by 2150 taking into account the likely growth in World population and the amount of energy each of us will consume. The estimate is required on a global basis which can be obtained by adding together the requirements of the individual countries and regions. It is important to remember that the final figure is an estimate – it is based on a model which involves many assumptions and other people may well make different assumptions. I do not claim 100% accuracy but the conclusions are a useful indicator of the total amount of energy we will eventually need.

Total Energy Consumption

The chart below shows how our overall consumption of energy from different sources, including biomass and primary electricity, has grown in the last 200 years. The figures relate to total energy consumed and includes all the energy used to generate secondary electricity. In this chart the data for Primary Electricity, mostly nuclear and hydro at the moment,

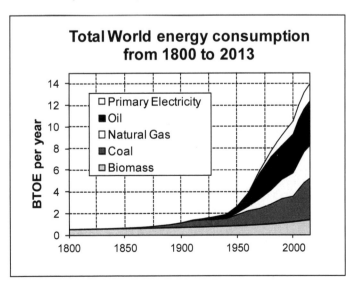

is based on the amount of energy which would have been required to generate this electricity from fossil fuels if it had not been generated directly. This allows us to see how much the consumption of fossil fuels has been reduced by the availability of this primary electricity.

In 1800 perhaps 10% of the fuel burned was converted into "useful" energy. When logs were burned to cook food most of the heat went up the chimney. Nowadays the "useful" proportion is more like 30% but still with the rest going up the chimney or being otherwise wasted or lost due to Carnot limitations. The total energy consumed has increased by a factor of 40 but the amount of useful energy has increased by a factor of perhaps 120. This means that even though the population has increased by a factor of about 10 over this period per capita availability of useful energy has itself increased by a factor of about 12. In future we are likely to continue improving the efficiency with which we use energy hence lowering the overall demand.

Sources Of Energy

The chart below shows the sources and overall application of energy in 2013. The overall total energy consumed was 13.7 BTOE. Of this 85% came from fossil fuels. Two thirds of this (59% of the total) was used directly to provide heat or drive transport etc while the remainder was used to generate electricity. Of the energy in the fossil fuels used to produce this secondary electricity, 62% goes up the chimney as smoke,

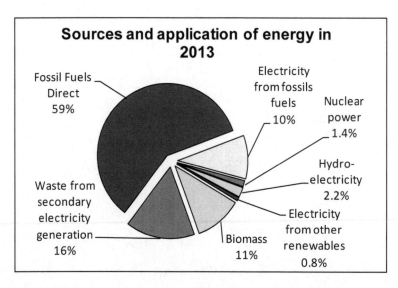

mostly as a result of the Carnot principle as discussed in Chapter 5. This waste during electricity generation account for 16% of our total energy consumption. As well as the electricity generated from fossil fuels there is also directly produced primary electricity. About a third of electricity comes from primary sources with 3.6% of the total coming from nuclear and hydro but with only 0.8% of the total coming from other renewable sources. The latter includes geothermal and solar energy as well as wind, wave and tidal power. At the moment these contribute a very small part of the total and in the future they will have to grow very considerably if they are to enable us to eliminate all use of fossil fuels. Development of these renewables is discussed in further detail in Chapter 10.

In addition to heat from fossil fuels and electricity from various sources over 10% of our energy now comes from biomass. In the past this was our only source of energy and wood and other dried vegetation was burned to heat houses and cook food and it was not until the industrial revolution that other sources of energy began to develop. Two thirds of the biomass used today is still used for cooking and heating in the Developing world but some is also being used in the Developed world, often in the form of wood chips, to run electrical power stations as well as heating homes. Other biomass is being used to produce biofuels which can be used to replace fossil fuels. This is particularly prevalent in Brazil where sugar cane is converted into methanol which can be used as a component in vehicle fuels but biofuels still account for only a small part of the overall total.

Even if we could treble our supply of renewable energy we could still not eliminate the use of fossil fuels. In the future we will need much more than this as overall demand for energy increases along with population and prosperity.

Which Regions Use Most Energy?

Consumption of energy in different parts of the World varies dramatically. Asia, which accounts for almost 60% of the World population consumes only 41% of the total while North America with 7% of the population, accounts for 20% of the energy used (i.e. the per capita consumption in North America is four times that in Asia as discussed below).

The chart below shows the twelve major energy users who between them account for almost 70% of consumption. Developed Countries appear in the top twelve because each individual person uses a lot of energy while some Developing Countries (China and India) appear in the list because they have so many people.

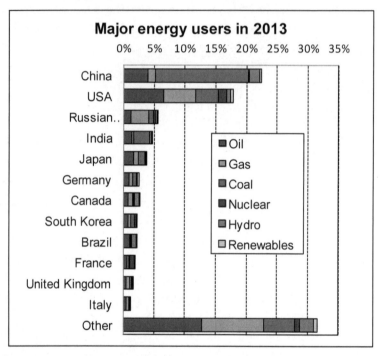

Per Capita Consumption

Total energy consumption is one measure of how energy use is changing but an alternative is per capita consumption, i.e. consumption per person. The next two charts show the trends in selected regions since 1950.

The first chart on the next page applies to Developed Countries. The per capita consumption in the Developed World is almost two and a half times the average for the World as a whole. Consumption in the USA is nearly double that in Europe and about four times the average for the World. There was some drop in consumption during the Iran-Iraq war as a result of price increases. This was more severe in the USA but it then levelled off although recent economic problems have caused a further, probably temporary, drop.

The second chart shows comparable figures for the Developing World. Per capita consumption is less than half the World average but for Africa and India it is about a third of this and only 6% of the level of consumption in the USA. In some countries, such as Bangladesh, the proportion is more than 40 times less than in the USA.

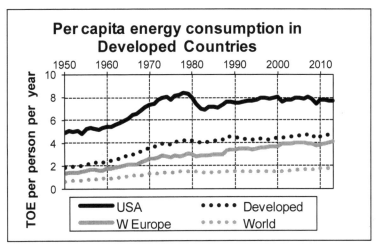

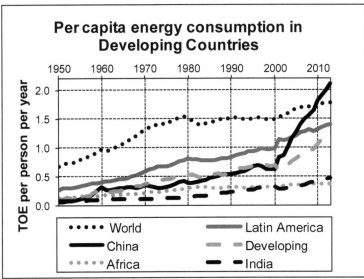

In the second chart the black line for China shows interesting trends. In 1950 consumption was among the lowest anywhere but there was steady growth until the mid nineties when political changes caused a temporary reduction. Since the start of the new millennium, however, growth has accelerated as the economic changes have worked their way through the system. This growth in China will have a significant impact on future World energy consumption. It will be absolutely essential for China to be included in the development of future global energy strategies. It is already the country with the highest total energy consumption and its share will go on rising as its per capita consumption increases still further.

The table on the right highlights the enormous differences between countries, with the average Canadian using nearly 60 times more energy (apart from physical labour) than his fellow citizen in Bangladesh. Unless we find alternatives the problem of Global Warming and exhaustion of reserves will be exacerbated as per capita consumption in countries such as China and India begins to catch up with that in the Developed World.

Energy consumption, per capita in 2013, in selected countries regions			
Group	TOE	Country	TOE
World Average	1.7	Canada	9.4
		USA	7.1
		Sweden	5.3
N America	7.3	Australia	4.9
Europe	3.2	Germany	4.0
S America	1.2	France	3.8
Asia	1.3	Japan	3.7
Africa	0.37	UK	3.1
		Italy	2.6
G8	5.3	South Africa	2.3
OECD	4.5	Portugal	2.3
		Hungary	2.1
Developed	5.1	China	2.1
NIC	1.5	Argentina	2.0
Developing	1.0	Brazil	1.4
Sub Sahara	0.16	India	0.48
		Bangladesh	0.17

Making Forecasts

As already seen there are wide differences between per capita consumption in Developed Countries and in Developing ones. Some countries, particularly the NICs (Newly Industrialized Countries) are beginning to catch up with the Developed World and per capita consumption in China is now just above the World average. There seems little doubt that consumption in the Developing World will continue to rise and we in the Developed World have no right to discourage poorer countries from aspiring to the standard of living we in the Developed World take for granted.

There is a some realisation in Developed Countries that we cannot continue to use so much energy and measures are at least being discussed to develop renewables. Under the Climate Change Act the government in the UK has set a target to reduce emissions in 2050 to 80% below the 1990 level so as to contribute towards limiting the global temperature rise to 2°C above the pre-industrial level. They have also established the Committee on Climate Change which set targets for reducing GHG emissions by 23% in 2012, by 29% by 2017, by 35% by 2022 and by 50% by 2027. The first target has already been met. There were also positive signs from some other Developed Countries at the UN Summit in September 2014.

The Four Scenarios

I have built a model to estimate World energy consumption over the next 150 years. Making projections 150 years ahead is taking outrageous liberties with my crystal ball but the results provide targets to aim at and they highlight the necessity of doing **something**.

Using the model, I have calculated the likely increase in consumption based on four scenarios. I have divided the World into seven regions and each scenario begins with the current per capita consumption of the region. Over time consumption moves gradually towards target values for each region with different targets for each scenario. In the model the per capita consumption will, by 2150, have moved 80% of the way from the current level towards the target values given in the table below.

Target values for Energy Consumption for Each Scenario	
Scenario	TOE/Capita
Status Quo	0.37
As World	1.7
Converging	3.5
As USA	8.0

Each scenario assumes that World population will also grow to a total of 10 billion as already discussed in Chapter 7. The scenarios are as follows:

Status Quo - per capita consumption in all the regions remains unchanged from the present levels.

As USA - at the other end of the scale this scenario assumes that consumption in all regions increases steadily towards a level of 8.0 TOE per capita, close to the current level in the US.

As World - assumes that everyone moves towards the current average World consumption of 1.7 TOE per capita. While this would help the poorer nations it would mean a dramatic 75% cut in North American energy consumption and a 50% cut in Europe. Such reductions would be extremely difficult to sell to people in the Developed World.

Converging - is similar but with everyone moving towards a target figure of 3.5 TOE per capita, close to the present consumption in Europe. This would be of particular benefit to the poorest regions with all of them ending up close to the new World average of 2.7 TOE per capita by 2150. It would also necessitate a 45% reduction of consumption in the USA, which would not be easy to sell to the American public.

Forecasts of World energy consumption over the next 150 years based on each scenario are shown in the chart below. Note that even under the Status Quo scenario consumption increases due to the rise in population. Under the Converging scenario total consumption in 2150 is up by a factor of almost three compared to current levels but under As USA it increases almost seven times.

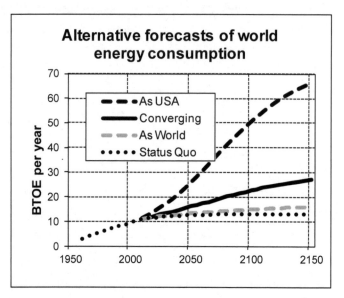

There is an important point that I have to reiterate. These forecasts are of the energy **WE WOULD LIKE TO HAVE** based on a fairer distribution of availability between regions. The forecasts assume we use energy as we do now and no allowance has been made for increases in efficiency. Unless we develop alternatives we are unlikely to have as much as we would like! These figures are certainly not set in stone but they do indicate target levels we have to aim for in the supply of alternatives.

The table on the next page shows per capita consumption in 2150 in each region for each of the four scenarios. From the Converging scenario consumption in the poorest regions, Africa and India, will be up by a factor of between four and six compared to current levels and will be about 70% of current consumption in Europe. The most contentious figure is the target for North America where per capita consumption would drop by over 40% to meet the target set by the converging scenario.

Per capita energy consumption in 2150 for each scenario (TOE)				
Region	Scenario			
	Status Quo	As World	Converging (Preferred)	As USA
Africa	0.4	1.5	2.5	6.6
Europe	3.7	2.1	3.5	7.2
S America	1.2	1.6	2.7	6.8
N America	8.1	2.8	4.7	8.0
Asia Pacific	1.5	1.7	2.7	6.8
China	1.2	1.6	2.7	6.8
India	0.4	1.5	2.5	6.6
World Average	**1.3**	**1.6**	**2.7**	**6.8**

In the remainder of this book I have used the Converging scenario as the "Preferred" one and refer to it as such. This is not intended as a rigid target for all time but it helps to define some realistic objectives.

Exhaustion Of Reserves

In Chapter 4 I looked at the level of current reserves of fossil fuels. I have now calculated the cumulative consumption of fossil fuels from today until 2300 for each scenario assuming that supplies are not limited. The results are shown in the chart on the next page. When cumulative consumption exceeds the total reserves we will have run out of fossil fuel. The current level of "Proven Reserves" is shown by the dashed horizontal line. The date when this line crosses the other lines is when reserves will run out for each scenario.

The current level of reserves is, of course, uncertain and there are continuing discoveries as well as economic developments which will make more reserves viable. There are those who argue that actual reserves may turn out to be four, or even five times greater than current estimates. The value for "All Reserves" is shown by the solid horizontal line. These reserves include the Athabasca tar sands, heavy oil in the Orinoco Valley and shale gas in many places which may be recovered through fracking.

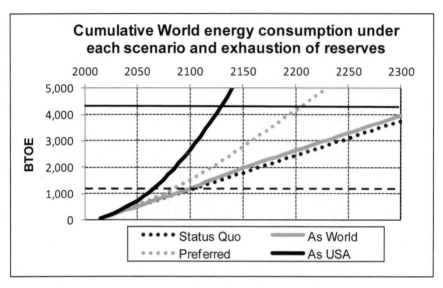

Expiry dates, taken from the chart, for each scenario are shown in the table below, both for "Proven Reserves" and for "All Reserves". The former is almost certainly over-cautious while the latter is probably over-optimistic.

Expiry dates for fossil fuels under each scenario				
Reserves	Scenario			
	Status Quo	As World	Preferred	As USA
"Proven Reserves" of Fossil fuels will be exhausted by	2100	2100	2080	2060
"All Reserves" of Fossil fuels will be exhausted by	2340	2320	2210	2140

Although artificial, the estimated date of 2080 for the expiry of fossil fuels for the Preferred Scenario does illustrate the urgency of the need to find alternatives, simply because we may run out of fossil fuels. Even if the "All Reserves" figure is the right one, we will still run out of fossil fuels in about 200 years.

This book is concerned with energy but don't forget that there are also reserves of other materials which will eventually run out and we need to be particularly careful in our use of some of the less common metals.

Who Will Use The Energy?

The next chart illustrates the proportions of total energy currently used by each region and the amounts they will use in 2150 under each of the scenarios. At present Europe and North America each account for about a quarter of total consumption. Under all the scenarios except "Status Quo" these proportions will have dropped dramatically by 2150 while the proportion consumed in Africa and India will have increased correspondingly.

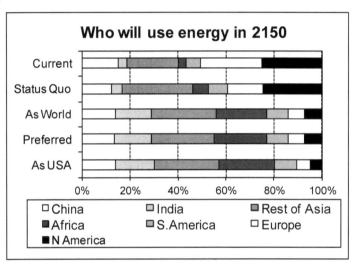

The Consequences

If all the additional energy demanded by the "As USA" scenario were to come from fossil fuels then CO_2 levels would rise by a factor of almost five by 2150. This is shown in the chart on the next page together with figures for two other scenarios. Even the Status Quo option doubles CO_2 levels and the preferred option will increase it by a factor of two and a half.

The second chart on the next page shows how the forecast CO_2 levels for each scenario would affect the global temperature. The worst case, "As USA", increases the average temperature in 2150 by 20°C above the level in 2000. The other scenarios predict increases of between 6°C and 10°C. These forecasts are only rough estimates and if rises of this magnitude were allowed to happen then many other factors would come into play which could substantially influence the actual values.

So far we have had a temperature rise of about 1°C in the last 150 years but most experts agree that this has already brought about changes in the climate. We are already beginning to feel the effects of only a 1°C rise, so **imagine what 10°C or more might do.**

We urgently need policies which encourage us to use energy more efficiently, which will deliver significant amounts of renewable energy in the near future and which also acknowledge that resources around the World need to be shared more equally.

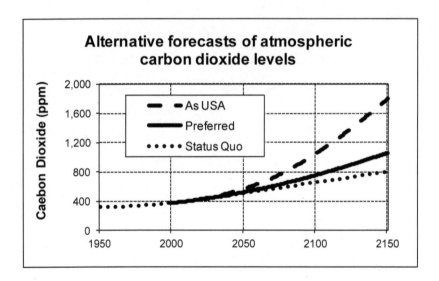

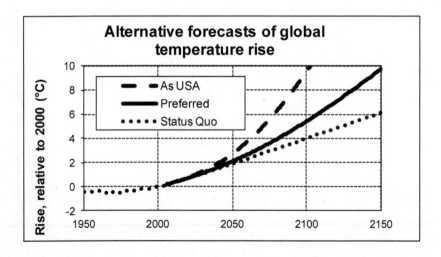

Targets

It is difficult to say with any precision what temperature rise[a] would be acceptable but it seems sensible to try to limit any further rise to another 2°C or, better still, to keep it below 1°C above the level in 2000. What will this mean in terms of the fossil fuels we will be able to use and the renewable replacements or the savings we will need to make?

In the next chart the top line shows the total demand for energy resulting from the Preferred Scenario before making any savings or increasing efficiency. The black area shows the fossil fuels we can burn and still keep the temperature rise below a further 1°C. If we also burn the fossil fuels represented by the white area then the temperature will rise by a further 2°C. The rest of the energy will have to come from what I am calling "alternatives" which are made up of carbon neutral renewable energy and savings which arise from a combination of the factors which were discussed for UK in Chapter 6. These factors include, among other things, better insulation, more efficient engines and motors, higher load factors in transport and avoidance of the waste associated with the generation of secondary electricity.

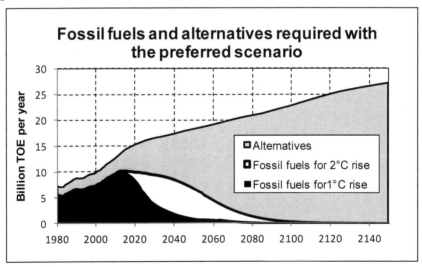

---

[a] The temperature rise from the beginning of the industrial revolution to the year 2000 was approximately 1°C. Future temperature rises are sometimes related to the beginning of the industrial revolution and sometimes to the current temperature. I refer to the rise above the current level so my figures are 1°C lower than some published figures.

To restrict the global temperature rise to a further 2°C then by 2030 we will have to cut our consumption of fossil fuels to about 90% of the present level which is equivalent to 60% the total energy likely to be needed by then. By 2050 the corresponding figures are about 60% and 40%. All burning of fossil fuels must cease before 2100.

To limit the future temperature rise to 1°C we will have to be much more stringent. By 2030 fossil fuel consumption must be no more that 30% of the current figure or 20% of the total. By 2050 both figures must be well under 10% and consumption of fossil fuels must be virtually eliminated by 2070.

At present only 3 BTOE/y of energy, less than 25% of the total, comes from renewables. The chart below shows that by 2050 we will need to be producing 12 BTOE/y of alternative energy to restrict the future temperature rise to further 2°C. To restrict the rise to 1°C the quantity increases to about 17 BTOE/y. By 2100 we will need 23 BTOE/y and by 2150 the figure for all alternatives is 27 BTOE/y. Remember, alternatives are a combination of savings and renewables.

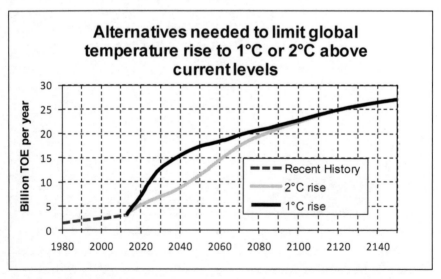

It is clear from the dashed grey line on the chart above that although the amount of renewables has increased a little over the last 30 years a much greater rate of increase will be needed over the next thirty years. By 2030, we will need at least four times as much alternative energy as we currently use to keep below the 1°C limit. We will need new sources or savings equivalent to four times the current output of all the existing hydroelectric and nuclear power plants plus the energy we now have from biomass. By 2050 the ratio will be five and by 2150 it will be almost ten. We have to begin very rapidly increasing our production of renewables or making major savings and we have to begin **NOW**. This really is a wake up call.

Where We Should Aim

In my view we should aim for the Preferred Scenario. This will lead to a fairer distribution of energy across the world by 2150 and there is a good chance of this being acceptable in most countries. The Developed World already has per capita consumption five times the World average. Under the proposed scenario then by 2150 per capita consumption in the rest of the World will be about two thirds that in the Developed World.

We should also aim to limit further temperature rise to 1°C. This will be hard to achieve but a difficult target may well spur us on to greater activity. The target for alternatives that we should aim for is the one illustrated by the solid black line in the chart on the previous page.

It would be easy for experts to argue with the details of the figures above but the principle conclusions are robust and, most importantly, they define the scale of the problem. Only if we have some idea of the scale can we form an opinion about the possible relevance of particular options which might contribute to a solution.

Savings We Can Make

According to this target then by 2150 we will need 27 BTOE of energy annually assuming the energy is used with the same efficiency as at present. To limit temperature rise to a further 1°C we need to make savings by using energy more efficiently and then provide all the rest that we need from renewable, carbon neutral sources.

Some of our electricity is already from primary sources, mostly hydro and nuclear power. The rest is secondary energy which comes from the burning of fossil fuels, a process which is only 38% efficient as was discussed in Chapter 5. This processes cannot be made more efficient because of the Carnot principle but if all our electricity comes from primary sources, as it must in the future, total energy demand will immediately be reduced by 20% as these losses will be avoided.

101

The chart below shows how the current use of energy around the World is divided, after excluding the saving resulting from electricity generation discussed above. Use is divided between transport applications and all non-transport uses which include heating and lighting as well as manufacturing and other miscellaneous uses.

Based on the discussion of UK energy use covered in Chapter 6, I have then estimated the level of saving which might reasonably be achieved across the world. For air and marine travel a 20% saving can be achieved by improved engine design, larger ships and aircraft, better routing and higher load factors. I have assumed the same figure for non-transport applications which will be achieved by improved insulation, with better heating and ventilation systems and the use of low energy lighting as well as making better use of waste heat in appropriate situations.

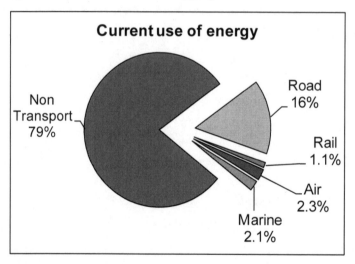

At the moment rail accounts for about 8% of travel on land. This will increase to 30% aided by more frequent services, reduced journey times, longer trains and appropriate pricing and subsidies. Fuel consumption per passenger on individual trains will improve by 30% as a result of higher load factors and improved designs. Because of the move from road to rail there will be less travel by car and the fuel consumption of the remaining vehicles will improve by 40%. This will be achieved by making cars smaller and increasing load factors.

Following the assumptions used for the UK in Chapter 6 I have estimated potential global savings. These will take place gradually and in the chart below the light grey area shows how these savings might grow. The black area shows the maximum consumption of fossil fuels compatible with a 1°C temperature rise and the white area shows the additional fossil fuels which could be consumed for a 2°C rise. The balance of the energy, shown by the dark grey area will have to come from renewables, the technology for much of which still has to be developed. The renewables needed to limit the rise to 2°C are shown by the dark grey area. To further limit the rise to only 1°C the energy covered by the white area will also have to come from renewables. After allowing for the savings discussed earlier, then by 2150 the world will need 17 BTOE of energy each year from renewable sources in order to keep the temperature steady.

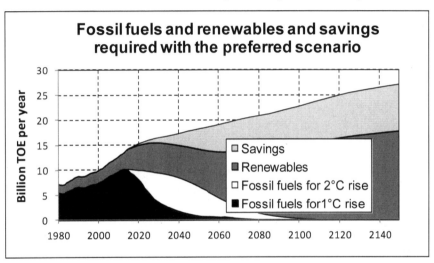

Portable and Static Energy

We use energy for heat and light, for transport and for running electric motors in appliances and other equipment as well as for electronics and for industrial processes. For the purposes of this discussion I have classified energy into two broad types, static and portable.

Static energy is what we use when we are stationary so we can be permanently connected to an energy source such as the gas main or the electricity grid. At present static energy is mostly provided in Developed Countries by a mixture of electricity and gas. In less Developed Countries much of it may come from coal or oil or from biomass. Almost all our static energy could come from electricity if enough of it were available.

Indeed, in the future most of it will come from electricity although some will also come from geothermal or from solar thermal sources.

Travel by road, rail, air or sea all require energy and this is usually in a portable form which is carried along with the passengers or freight. Today portable energy is almost entirely supplied in the form of oil products derived from fossil fuels but in the future this could be replaced with biofuels or other synthetic products or by batteries.

Road transport currently relies almost entirely on oil although smaller vehicles can be battery powered. Developments in the future are likely to make batteries smaller, lighter and cheaper. Hydrogen, generated using electricity, can also be regarded as a portable fuel but again with limitations although it may become a more realistic option for small land vehicles in the future. This is already possible using high pressure gas cylinders but in future hydrogen may be absorbed onto special solid pellets which can be recycled after use. Remember that battery power and hydrogen will only be carbon neutral when the electricity involved in charging batteries or producing hydrogen comes entirely from carbon neutral sources.

In addition ideas are being developed in which hydrogen and CO_2 are converted into methanol, ethanol or perhaps other hydrocarbons. These can then be used as liquid fuels for transport. It is potentially possible to do this at present using CO_2 extracted from the flue gases of fossil fuel power stations. Work is going on to develop suitable carbon capture processes but these will only be viable as long as fossil fuels are being used. Processes are also under investigation in which CO_2 will be absorbed directly from the normal atmosphere and sunlight is then used to combine it with water to produce methanol which can be used as portable energy. Such processes are a long way from being economically viable but they are certainly a possibility.

Rail transport uses a mix of oil and electricity. Electric trains or trams use electricity by connecting to the grid or their own generating system and in the future the proportion of electric power could increase considerably otherwise biofuels or possibly hydrogen will need to be used.

Today sea and air transport both rely entirely on oil for their energy. It is difficult to imagine any alternative in the future for air transport. Aircraft powered by battery-driven propellers do not seem very realistic. Similarly oil is likely to remain the most likely fuel for marine transport. Once fossil fuels have become unacceptable the most obvious source of fuel for sea and air transport will be oil equivalents produced from biomass although hydrogen absorbed onto pellets may be a possibility. Synthetics, made from the combination of water and CO_2 from the atmosphere are also a possibility.

To look at how we can meet future energy needs it is useful to split forecasts of energy demand into static and portable. Portable fuels will come mainly from biofuels although in the long run hydrogen is a possibility. The split between use of the two types of energy is based on the following assumptions:

- road transport starts off with 100% of portable fuel but this steadily reduces to 50% as batteries become more efficient. This change is virtually complete by 2080
- rail transport starts with 80% of trains using portable fuel but this steadily reduces to 20% as more and more tracks are electrified. This change is also virtually complete by 2080
- all air and marine applications continue to use 100% portable fuels.

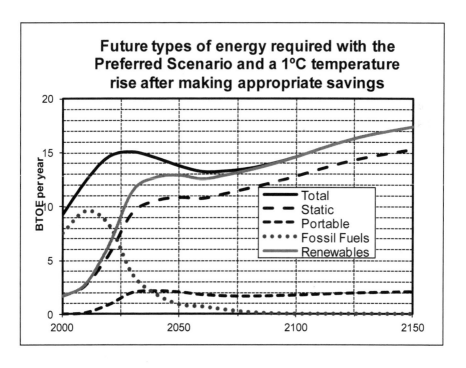

Based on these assumptions and the split between the applications shown earlier the demand for portable and static renewables has been calculated. The chart on the previous page shows the results. Use of fossil fuels drops to virtually zero by 2075. We already get some of our static energy from renewable hydro and nuclear power and the total increases steadily reaching 15 BTOE per year by 2150. At the moment all our portable transport fuel comes from fossil fuels. As use of these is suppressed we begin to need renewable, portable energy with demand reaching 2 BTOE per year by 2150 leading to a total energy demand for renewables of 17 BTOE per year after making the savings previously discussed.

Long Term Energy Consumption

Earlier we have talked about per capita energy consumption without taking into account savings we can make through lifestyle changes and improvements in efficiency. On this basis global demand for energy was projected to be 27 BTOE per year by 2150. With a World population of 10 billion, per capita consumption would be 2.7 BTOE per year.

After taking into account the savings which can realistically be made my estimated forecast of global energy consumption in 2150 is 17 BTOE per year as discussed earlier in this chapter. This is equivalent to a per capita consumption of 1.7 TOE. It is important to remember that this reduction in per capita consumption, relative to earlier estimates, is due to savings and improvements in efficiency and does not imply any overall reduction in the availability of useful energy. It also allows for the fact that all electricity comes from primary sources and the waste associated with the generation of secondary electricity is avoided.

In the chart on the previous page the total line shows the overall amount of energy which will be required annually up to 2150. It also shows the amount which will be needed in static and portable forms. In addition the chart shows the amount of energy which can come from fossil fuels as well as the renewables needed to limit the future temperature rise to a further 1°C. The use of fossil fuels will have to fall to zero well before 2100.

Chapter 10

Renewable Energy

How Energy Much Will We Need?

The chart below shows how consumption of energy has increased from 1980 up to the present time, relative to the forecast nett demand in 2050 after subtracting the energy lost when fossil fuels are used to generate secondary electricity. As you will see the rate of increase has been fairly steady. We are now almost half way from 1980 to 2050 and nett demand for energy will continue rising over the next thirty five years, though slightly less rapidly than in the past, but only so long as we make the savings I have suggested are feasible.

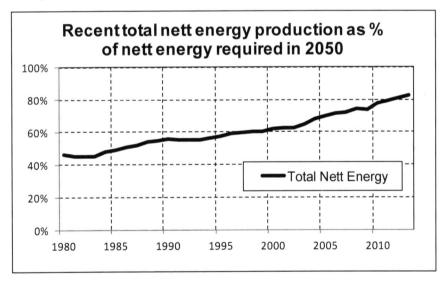

To limit Global Warming we need to control the emission of GHGs and eventually reduce the use of fossil fuels to zero while at the same time supplying the necessary energy from carbon neutral sources. This chapter is concerned with where the necessary renewables will come from.

After making appropriate savings, the global demand for energy by 2150 will be 17 BTOE per year according to my Preferred Scenario, as discussed in the last chapter. By that date all of our energy will need to come from renewable sources. The table summarises the amount of renewable, carbon neutral, energy which will be needed at various dates in the future to limit temperature rise to a further 1°C or 2°C. The figures have been estimated after allowing

Renewable energy needed to limit Global Warming		
	BTOE/year	
	1°C Rise	2°C Rise
2030	12	6
2050	13	7
2100	15	15
2150	17	17

for savings which can be made and after realistic improvements in efficiency have been achieved. The figures also assume that only primary electricity is used. Note that, in the end, the same amount of renewables will be needed, irrespective of the target temperature rise, as all fossil fuels must be replaced well before 2100.

Recent Production Of Renewables

The chart below shows how production of renewables has increased since 1980. There has been a steady increase up to 2013, but perhaps surprisingly, in view of the recent publicity about global warming, there has been no recent acceleration in the production of renewables.

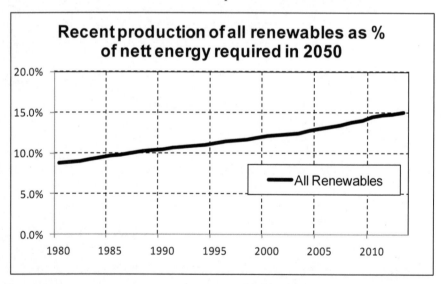

In 1980 the World produced 1.3 BTOE of renewable energy. By 2013 the amount had increased by 0.8 BTOE to a total of 2.1 BTOE, an increase of only 0.025 BTOE per year. To keep the temperature rise to 1°C above the current level the production of renewables will have to increase by a further 11 BTOE by 2050 taking the total to 13 BTOE. This will require an annual increase in renewables of 0.3 BTOE per year – this is 12 times faster than they have been increasing since 1980. To limit the temperature rise to 2°C production "only" needs to increase 5 times faster than it has since 1980 to take the total to 7 BTOE per year. These figures of 12 and 5 are averages over the period from now up to 2050 but we really need even higher acceleration in production between now and 2030.

We really must wake up. Globally we have to take development of renewables energy very much more seriously than we have been doing recently. We have to begin major developments **IMMEDIATLY.** Much of the progress will come from an accumulation of many very small projects. For example a BioBus, travelling between Bath and Bristol in the UK, has just been launched. This runs on methane generated by processing human waste. We need many, many more projects such as this to be implemented.

The Different Types Of Renewables

Today almost 15% of our energy comes from renewables, primarily biomass, hydroelectricity and nuclear power. There are a number of types of renewables which will have to be developed to meet the future demand. These include:

- Biomass
- Hydroelectricity
- Nuclear Power
- Wind Power
- Solar Electricity and Heat

- Geothermal Energy
- Wave Power
- Tidal Power
- Synthetic Fuels

The next chart shows the contribution of each of these types of energy to the current overall supply of renewables. It is clear that Biomass makes

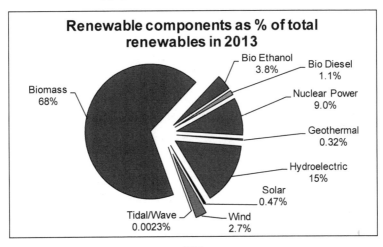

by far the largest contribution and it is perhaps surprising that the contribution of wind and particularly solar power is so small despite the publicity these options frequently attract.

This rest of this chapter is devoted to a review of each of these sources with a look at how they have grown in the past and how much each might contribute to global energy demand in the future.

The Potential Of Each Energy Source

To harvest the required amount of renewable energy will need a great deal of manufacturing, engineering and construction as well as technological development. This may be expensive but the cost will be offset by the fact that we will no longer need to continue exploring for oil or gas, to operate refineries or to transport the products. In the end, economics will have a considerable impact on which of the renewable sources take off most quickly and it is in this area that technological developments can have a significant impact. The economics will be strongly affected by the technical developments which take place and as these are unpredictable so too are the economics. The following discussion is concerned with what is, or may become possible, **not with what is cheapest now**. Future discoveries and developments will have a substantial impact on the relative amounts of energy coming from different sources.

I can make a guess at the amount of energy it may be feasible to produce from a particular source but it is more difficult to estimate how quickly that source will develop. I have already highlighted the need to develop renewables very quickly and that applies to all the options but I have not attempted to forecast how quickly each will develop. The crucial fact is that overall, renewable energy production must increase very rapidly.

- Biomass

Biomass was for a long time our only source of energy until the invention of water wheels and the discovery of fossil fuels. It is still the main source of energy in many villages in Developing countries and biofuels are significant in the modern world. Biofuels are produced from plants. These plants are often naturally occurring but increasingly crops are grown specifically for the purpose. The chart on the next page shows the contribution biomass has made to our energy needs over the last thirty years as a percentage of the nett energy which will be required in 2050. There has been a very slow growth which must accelerate in the future.

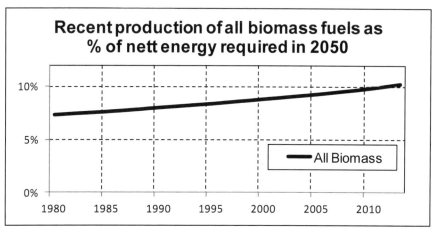

We produce biofuels from crops and some of these are grown specifically for the purpose. Some crop varieties already give high yields but in the future there will be improvements in the crops used giving even higher yields. Development of these new varieties may involve genetic engineering. There will also be improvements in cultivation methods and it may become possible to grow crops, with acceptable yields, in less fertile areas. There will also be improvements in the methods used to convert the raw biomass into useful energy products.

We already make bioethanol and biodiesel from crops but when used in road vehicles, they are at present heavily diluted with fossil fuels. Civil aircraft have already been flown using a proportion of biofuel and military flights have been made with 100% biofuel. The chart below shows how rapidly production of these biofuels has accelerated in the last twenty

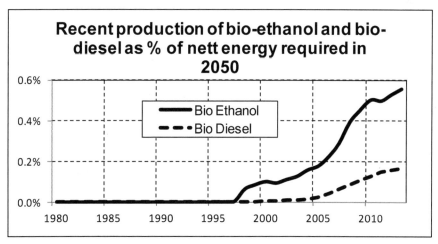

years. However, they still represent less than a tenth of the total biomass used and only a small amount of total energy consumption but they could become much more significant. In the future we will need to make biofuels which can be used in existing engines without dilution or to develop engines which accept fuels with different properties. Biofuels are likely to become the main source of portable energy for use in transport.

Many of the crops such as corn (maize) or soya have poor yields of biofuels but sugar cane or palm oil can produce more than ten times as much fuel per hectare. Other crops such as switch grass or moringa could become significant. The biggest challenge is to grow biofuels in parallel with food crops so that as well as providing energy there is enough food for everyone on the planet. Growing all the food and fuel needed while also preserving biodiversity may present other major challenges. This should be possible but will require considerable international cooperation.

The total calorific value of the food produced per hectare is considerably more when growing vegetables than when producing meat. The ratio for corn to beef is about 10:1. If we all became vegetarian then we would need less land to produce our calories and we would have more available for biofuels. Overall it is more complicated than this as there are other essential nutrients not easily obtained from vegetables. Furthermore, animals can live, at least in part, on waste products and some of the land used for rearing animals is not very suitable for arable purposes.

The green layer near the surface of stagnant ponds usually consists of algae. Algae are a large and diverse group of simple plants which grow floating in water. It is possible that effective methods will be found for growing algae on a commercial scale. This has the potential for producing algal biofuels on a significant scale using either inland waters or coastal areas close to land. Such production may, of course, have significant adverse environmental effects in some situations. On the other hand experiments are underway to see if algae can remove the toxic metals from the waste water of tin mines in Cornwall. If successful this will recover significant amounts of rare elements as well as producing biofuel and pure water – a win-win result which could be applied around the world.

Hydroponics are also a possibility. This is where crops are grown in an industrial plant without soil but with plenty of light. The temperature is optimised and the roots are in water containing the necessary nutrients. Such processes can, in principle, produce very high yields of biomass.

After allowing for the land needed to feed the World's 10 billion people in 2150, there could still be suffcent land to produce 2.8 BTOE per year of biofuels with the help of fertilizer. This estimate is nett of the energy needed to grow, harvest and process the crops and is about double the energy we currently get from these sources.

- Hydroelectric Power

Hydroelectric power relies on water in a reservoir at the top of a hill running down to the sea via a turbine which converts some of its potential energy into mechanical power, which can then, among other things be used to generate electricity. The water in the sea evaporates to form clouds. These produce rain which refills the reservoirs and so the cycle repeats itself. Apart from biofuels this is the renewable energy which has been in use for the greatest length of time and, as can be seen in the chart below, it already makes a significant contribution to our energy supply. We know how to do it and a number of large projects are already in operation and there are also many micro systems around the world.

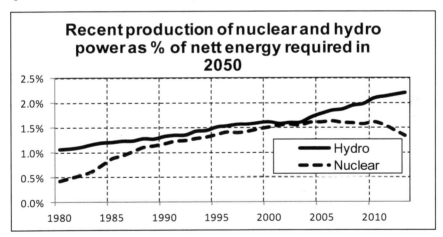

Hydroelectricity makes a significant contribution to the World energy supply. Current output is 0.27 BTOE per year and is concentrated in a few countries with the largest producers being China, Brazil, Canada and the USA. There is considerable additional potential, including micro systems, which could be developed and which will gradually become more economically viable. In the future even larger projects may be needed and they may become part of pumped storage schemes.

There can be environmental problems with hydroelectricity which often necessitates the flooding of large areas of land and it may involve relocation of substantial numbers of people. There can also be flooding of certain wild life habitats and rivers can become less navigable. Taking these factors into account, this source has the potential to meet between 7% and 10% of energy demand in 2150 or a total of about 1.5 BTOE per year of electricity. This is five to six times the amount of hydropower currently used.

- Nuclear Power

It is arguable that nuclear power is not renewable since the fuels it runs on are finite. However, I include it among the other types of renewables because it is carbon neutral.

Nuclear power has been produced for over 50 years and there are more than 400 nuclear power stations currently in operation. As well a Hydro Power the chart on the previous page also shows the contribution of Nuclear Power to the global energy supply. It had been growing steadily but the rate of growth began to fall in 2000 and there was a substantial drop after the Fukushima disaster in 2011. Since then Germany has also started switching away from nuclear power.

Availability of uranium for reactors is finite and with current technology, it will run out in a relatively short time. Fast breeder reactors generate up to fifty times more electricity from the same amount of uranium. These are close to being operational but they do raise some extra security questions. If fast breeders are put into operation, they will be able to supply substantial amounts of electricity for a very long time.

The oceans contain small traces of uranium and if methods of recovering this can be developed, we would have another vast pool of potential fuel. Hydrogen/deuterium fusion is a tantalizing possibility and if it can ever be made to work, it would solve all our energy needs for many thousands of years. There might also be other nuclear processes not yet dreamed of which might be developed to satisfy our needs.

If fast breeder reactors are adopted, then the potential would increase by a factor of 50 and reserves would last much longer. If fusion technology can be made to work much more power will be available but considerable technical developments will be needed before this becomes possible.

Thorium is another potential nuclear fuel and it is four or five times more prevalent than Uranium. Even with today's technology it has the potential to produce as much power per tonne of fuel as a Generation IV reactor using uranium even though thorium reactors are not yet fully developed. India has about 25% of the known reserves of thorium and already has a nuclear plant operating with it at Kakrapar and the Indians are developing an Advanced Heavy Water Reactor which will soon be operational. By 2030 India plans to generate 30% of its electricity from thorium. As with uranium, by-products from thorium reactors can be used in nuclear weapons but in other respects thorium is safer than uranium as it produces much smaller quantities of long lived radioactive waste.

Nuclear power presents some risks but if these are considered acceptable, after putting into place good safety and security measures, it can make a significant contribution to the total energy supply. Nuclear power already contributes about 2% to the World energy supply. At current rates of consumption proven, commercially viable, reserves will only last for another 70 years. However, there are considerable additional reserves including the oceans. These could well become available and would allow the contribution of nuclear power to increase gradually until accounting for 8% of our energy supply or 1.4 BTOE per year – this is six or seven times as much nuclear power as we use at present. On this basis probable reserves would last for only another 150 years but by then other technology is likely to be available.

- Wind Power

Wind can be used to drive windmills and in the past these were used directly to grind corn or drive machinery. Wind energy is now used almost exclusively to generate electricity. We know how to build turbines and there are already some very large ones in operation. The chart on the next page shows the contribution of wind power to the global energy supply. There has been considerable growth in wind power since 2000 but it still accounts for only a small proportion of the total energy supply which is perhaps surprising in view of the publicity it receives.

There are unlikely to be major changes in the way the turbines operate but there will be improvements in detailed design which will increase efficiency. Such developments are unlikely to eliminate noise but there will be improvements in materials so that the turbines will last longer. The main technical developments will be concerned with adapting the structure for different locations. We already have turbines on land and in shallow water. In the future, we are likely to have floating turbines which may be some distance out at sea. Development of these will considerably increase the overall amount of wind energy which can be harvested.

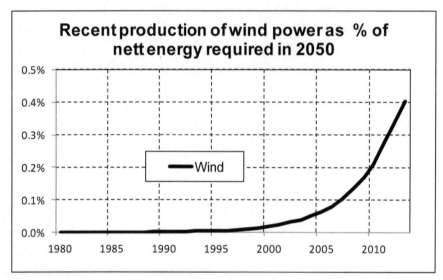

Perhaps the biggest problem will be the impact on the environment. People frequently object both to the noise and to the visual presence of turbines and we will need to minimise this impact as far as we can. However, these are problems which we shall have to learn to accept, as indeed, we have learnt to accept many other changes to our environment since the onset of the industrial revolution.

Wind power has the greatest potential of any of the renewable sources but it is variable and erratic. Overall there are perhaps 54 BTOE per year of harvestable wind energy, mostly on land but a third in near shore locations. Other environmental considerations and distance from where it is needed limit the amount which can realistically be used.

Technically, we can have a very substantial amount of wind power if we are prepared to accept the impact on the local environment. Perhaps a bigger problem is the high initial cost even though running costs are very low. Based on the use of 20% of nearshore sites and 5% of land sites it is estimated that wind power could generate the equivalent of 5.4 BTOE per year of electrical energy. This is a massive increase by a factor of 100 compared to the wind power currently generated.

- Solar Energy

The most obvious source of renewable energy is sunlight. On average the solar energy hitting the Earth's atmosphere is equal to twelve and a half thousand times the energy currently consumed by the Human race or to put it another way it is equivalent to the output of a large power station for every fifty people alive on the planet.

Solar heat for hot water on a domestic scale is already fairly efficient and there is no obvious area where a breakthrough is likely to happen. On a large scale, solar heat can be used to produce steam and thus to generate electricity in turbines. This is achieved using mirrors or lenses which track the Sun and focus the energy onto a small area. As a result, much higher temperatures can be reached thus producing steam with which to generate electricity. The hotter the steam the more efficient the process. Again, we know how to do this although, in the future, mirrors and lenses will improve and we will, to some extent, be able to improve the efficiency of the turbines.

Electricity is already produced directly through photovoltaic panels both on a domestic scale and in very large plants. As you would expect, the process is more effective in areas with a high intensity of sunlight. The nearer you are to the tropics, the more Sun you get and the less the seasonal fluctuations. Again, we have the technology but there is scope for improving the efficiency of solar PV panels. At present up to 20% of the light hitting the panel can be converted to electricity. Experimental panels have been made with an efficiency of over 40% but they are expensive at present and involve rare elements to make them effective. It is possible that in the future the efficiency of panels will improve up to perhaps 35% and it may be possible to make them with less rare elements.

On a domestic scale, if every household worldwide had $10m^2$ of panels and their efficiency increased to about 35%, this would contribute 0.6 BTOE per year. Such panels can be developed to produce either electricity or hot water.

There are a very small number of existing large scale solar plants in operation for generation of electricity through either PV panels or production of steam. Steam can also be used for other industrial purposes. If the number of existing plants can be multiplied by a factor of 500 then this would produce 0.9 BTOE of energy per year.

Since the intensity of sunlight varies with the seasons, the weather and the time of day we must also be able to store energy so that we can use it at our convenience. Small scale systems can store energy in batteries or as hot water and large scale plant can be designed to store heat during the day to generate electricity at other times. Storage will get round some of the daily imbalance of supply and demand but cannot solve the problem of seasonal variations, particularly in areas away from the tropics. Overall we might get a total of 1.5 BTOE per year from solar power as heat or electricity.

The chart below shows how harvesting of solar power has increased over the last thirty years. Until 2005 there was very little production but since then output has increased by a factor of thirty and it looks like it will carry on rising although it is still only a very, very small part of the total.

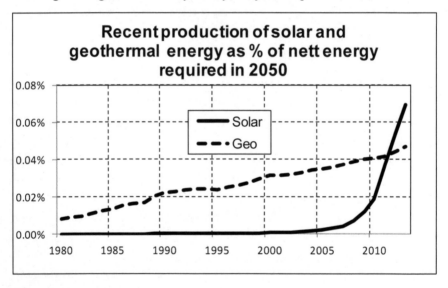

- Geothermal Heat

As well as showing data for solar energy the chart above also shows how our use geothermal energy, which we extract from the ground beneath us, has increased. The core of the Earth is very hot, about 7,000 °C at the centre. The top layer of the surface is a vast store for the energy which flows up to it from the centre and which can be harvested with heat pumps. Heat pumps operate like fridges but in reverse. They take a large volume of a warm liquid and turn it into a smaller volume of a hotter liquid. In areas of low population density the energy can be extracted from the top few metres of the Earth's surface but where the population density is higher it may be necessary to go down a hundred metres or so to get to a higher temperature and hence extract more energy from the same area of land. The process normally creates relatively low temperatures and is only suitable for heating or producing hot water. It does not provide electricity.

Geothermal heat is already used to a limited extent on a domestic scale providing heating and hot water. There may be minor improvements in efficiency but we already have the technology including the necessary heat pumps. When we go deeper for the heat there may be improvements which could be made in drilling techniques.

Taking into account the fact that two thirds of the World's population live in the tropics where space heating is rarely needed then the geothermal heat may eventually provide only about 10% of the energy required globally. This is equal to 1.7 BTOE of energy per year.

- Geothermal Electricity

Geothermal electricity relies on using geothermal heat to produce high temperature steam. Normally the temperature of the Earth's crust rises by 25-30°C for every kilometre you go down. To generate electricity you need steam above 300°C which would mean drilling down 10 km. Although this is possible and some oil wells go deeper than this it cannot, at present, be done on the scale required to drive a power station.

There are, however, some locations where the temperature rise is much more rapid and indeed there are a few places where steam emerges naturally at the surface. The greatest potential is around the rim of the Pacific, the so called "Ring of Fire" as well as in the Mediterranean and down through the middle of Africa, in Iceland and in New Zealand. A number of plants already operate in these areas so the technology exists and output could certainly be expanded. Developments in deep drilling and methods of cracking the rocks way down in the crust will increase the range of locations where geothermal electricity is a feasible option.

Currently geothermal electricity accounts for only 0.05% of the World's energy supply but this could rise to perhaps 10%. This is the equivalent of 1.7 BTOE per year of electricity. Geothermal energy has the considerable advantage that it is available 24/7 and is not subject to daily or seasonal variations. Overall we will need to increase the amount harvested in the future by a factor of two or three hundred.

- Wave Power

Wave power relies on the energy in waves created by the wind blowing across the oceans and this too can be converted into electricity. Wave power is available across all the World's oceans but it can only be harvested at reasonable cost from close to the shore and particularly where a prevailing wind blows over a long distance towards that shore thus increasing the height of the waves.

Wave power is in its infancy and there is little doubt that there will be significant improvements in the amount of energy which can be recovered. Current models float on the surface and the power is generated as their components bend and flex relative to each other. Generators can also be moored to the seabed generating electricity as they move up and down. There is scope for development which may make wave power more competitive.

Although it is subject to changes in the weather and to some seasonal variation, locations can be found which produce a fairly constant output of energy. Wave power can interfere with shipping and can have an impact on marine life but this is usually manageable although it may limit the number of sites which are suitable. It is estimated that wave power could produce the equivalent of 1.4 BTOE per year of electricity but this would be an increase by a factor of a thousand or more over the energy currently generated from the waves.

- Tidal Power

Tidal power is only operational on a very small scale at present. The rise and fall between high and low tide levels varies considerably with location and tidal power is only applicable at a finite number of locations where the tidal range is at the upper end of the scale. This limits the number of suitable locations but we have the technology available if we choose to apply it and if we choose to accept its other, often significant, environmental effects. It has, for example, been suggested that the tide could be used to generate electricity in the UK in the Severn Estuary but this has raised much concern over the impact on the wetlands along the coast and the effect of this on local wildlife.

Availability of tidal energy varies on a regular and predictable pattern. Tidal power usually involves building dams and this can lead to destruction of wild life habitats. At present there is only one significant plant in use but if all the dozen or so locations with the greatest potential were fully exploited, then something over 1% of World energy could come from this source by 2150. This is equivalent to 0.2 BTOE per year.

The chart below shows the recent amount of energy derived from tides and wave power. The amount generated is a very small proportion of the total but they both have the potential to become much more significant.

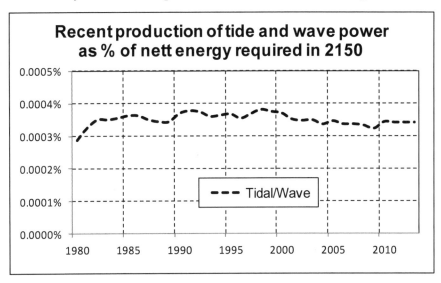

Synthetic Fuels

In this context, synthetic fuels are materials made to store energy from renewable sources. Such fuels are portable and have the potential for use in transport. The simplest synthetic fuel is hydrogen which is produced by electrolysis of water or by heating of hydrocarbons to high temperatures. It is important to remember that hydrogen is only carbon neutral if it is generated using renewable electricity. Hydrogen can be stored as a gas but high pressures are needed to store a useful amount in a reasonable volume and refuelling is difficult and can be dangerous.

There is an alternative to high pressure storage which may become a feasible, economic solution. Some materials absorb hydrogen at low temperatures and with the right substance the relative volume stored can be much higher than in a high pressure cylinder. The absorbent is produced in the form of small pellets and these are loaded with hydrogen. At the "filling station" these are put into the vehicle fuel tank. A flow of these is fed to a small heater where the hydrogen is released, as required, to run the engine. The exhausted pellets are then recycled at the next filling station.

Another way of storing hydrogen is as a component of methanol. A mixture of CO_2 and hydrogen, in the presence of a catalyst and at the right temperature can be converted to methanol according to the reaction:

$$CO_2 + 3H_2 = CH_3OH + H_2O$$

Hydrogen is produced by electrolysis using electricity generated from renewable sources. The obvious source of CO_2 is to extract it from the flue gases of a power station but that will only be possible while we are still burning fossil fuels to generate electricity. However, absorbents are being developed to extract CO_2 from the exhaust gases of vehicles. The absorbent can be collected from filling stations and returned when loaded with hydrogen.

Another method is to extract CO_2 from the atmosphere. This is thought to be possible, even though the CO_2 is only present at very low concentrations, so long as the humidity of the air is low. Such a plant could be set up anywhere around the World and does not need to be near to where the CO_2 was generated.

One of the problems with wind turbines and other sources of renewable electricity is that output is sporadic and peaks of availability do not match peaks in demand. The generation of hydrogen for production of methanol could use peaks of electricity when it is surplus to other requirements. Such peak lopping will become more and more important as we become increasingly dependent on renewable electricity.

Static And Portable Energy

Static and portable energy has already been discussed in Chapter 9. At present about a fifth of energy is used for transport, much of which requires "portable" energy which can be carried around in the vehicle concerned, whether it is an automobile, a truck, an aeroplane or a ship. Other forms of transport, particularly electric trains and trams, use electricity which is effectively static energy. By 2150 demand for portable energy will be about 2 BTOE per year which could just about be supplied by biofuels. However, synthetic fuels, as discussed above could reduce demand for biofuels and ease the pressure on land which is also needed to grow food.

Most of the rest of our energy use is "static" and much of it is supplied to us at home or in offices or factories through the gas or electricity mains. In the future most of this will be supplied as electricity with the rest being available directly as heat.

A factor to be taken into account in supplying energy is when and where it is needed. Solar power and wind, wave or tidal power are available in varying amounts in all parts of the World but they are also subject to considerable daily and seasonal variations. The long-term strategy needs to take into account methods of storing energy so that it can be made available, as discussed later, when and where it is needed.

Overall Development

There are a variety of renewable sources of energy and the amounts available from each source, as discussed above, are summarised in the table on the right. The total is just enough to meet the estimated demand in 2150. In many cases, we already have the technology to exploit these potential sources. Large-scale projects will be necessary involving complex engineering designs but there is nothing, except the will to do so and the cost, to stop us putting such principles into practice now.

Renewable energy potentially available from different sources	
	BTOE/yr
Solar heat + PV	1.5
Hydroelectric power	1.5
Wind power	5.4
Wave power	1.4
Tidal power	0.2
Geothermal heat	1.7
Geothermal electricity	1.5
Biofuels	2.8
Nuclear	1.4
TOTAL	17.4

Having said this, almost all processes can be improved and there will be detailed developments which will improve efficiency, increase longevity and reduce costs as well as changing the relative costs and benefits of competing systems. In a few cases fundamental research is necessary before they can be developed and there may be other solutions we have not yet dreamed of.

Overall there are many particular areas where research needs to focus. These include:

- development of crops with higher yields and better methods of extracting biofuels from them while maintaining biodiversity
- improving methods for fracturing rock strata for geothermal heat

- development of algal biofuels
- developing off shore floating wind turbines
- development of fast breeder nuclear reactors
- development of thorium reactors
- investigation of methods for extraction of uranium from low level ores or from the oceans
- feasibility of hydrogen fusion reactions
- improving the efficiency of solar PV panels
- increasing the efficiency of steam turbines
- developing new ideas for wave powered turbines
- developments of synthetic fuels particularly those using extraction of low concentrations of CO_2 from the atmosphere
- development of materials to increase the longevity of installations
- development of lighter, cheaper and less expensive batteries.

It is good to explore plenty of possibilities and although some of these will produce nothing useful others may turn out to be unexpectedly successful – no one can predict the outcome of research.

Availability Of Energy

We can conclude from the above that methods are available for obtaining all the energy the World will need in 2150 from renewable resources.

Some key characteristics of energy from different sources			
Source	Location	Variability	Type
Solar - domestic	Widespread	Daily/seasonally	Electricity/heat
Solar - large	Tropics	Daily/seasonally	Electricity/heat
Hydro	Widespread	As needed	Electricity
Wind	Land/near shore	Irregular	Electricity
Wave	Near shore	Irregular	Electricity
Tidal	Coast	Variable	Electricity
Geothermal - domestic	Widespread	As needed	Heat
Geothermal - large	Ring of fire etc.	As needed	Electricity/heat
Biofuels	Widespread	As needed	Transport
Synthetic fuels	Widespread	As needed	Transport
Nuclear	Widespread	As needed	Electricity/heat

However, availability of some forms of energy varies daily and seasonally or sometimes at random and it is often focussed in particular geographic regions. Demand for energy also varies with time of day, with the seasons and from place to place. We thus need a means of getting the energy from where it can be harvested to where it is needed and when it is needed. The table on the previous page summarises relevant characteristics of energy from different sources.

In this context, there are three types of energy:

- Electricity can satisfy most of our energy needs at home including heating, air conditioning, cooking and lighting. It can also meet many commercial and industrial needs and it can be converted into heat when needed. It can be used directly to drive trains and trams. Electricity is easy to transport over long distances using a high voltage grid. The chief drawback is that it can only be stored with difficulty. From the table you will see that geothermal, nuclear and hydro-electricity can be made available as needed with appropriate forward planning. Planning needs to be day to day rather than hour to hour as generators, particularly nuclear ones, cannot just be turned on and off at the drop of a hat. Availability of solar electricity varies in a regular manner while electricity from wind, waves or tide varies irregularly. There is also the possibility of synthetic fuels which can be used for transport and which can be made using peaks in electricity supply.

- Heat can be used directly for space heating or in industrial processes or it can be converted into electricity. Like electricity, it is difficult to store, but enough can sometimes be stored to even out supply and demand between day and night. However, unlike electricity it is also difficult to transport, unless converted to electricity. It needs to be used very close to where it is produced.

- Most biofuels are liquids which can easily be stored or transported. They are probably the only viable fuel for marine transport and aircraft and are also useful for both passenger and freight transport on land where electric trains or trams are not feasible. Although production of biofuels may well be seasonal, they can readily be stored and transported and can be made available as and when needed.

Apart from biofuels, energy is difficult to store but there are some options as follows:

- Electricity can be stored in batteries but these are small and expensive and at present have only limited use in small-scale applications. They can be used for small cars but these have a low top speed and only a limited range. Solar panels can be used to recharge batteries during the day to provide light at night.

- Electricity can be stored using pumped storage. When surplus electricity is available, it can be used to pump water uphill to a reservoir. It can then flow back down and through a hydroelectric turbine to produce electricity when it is needed. Pumped storage is feasible on a fairly large scale but at least 30% of the energy is lost in the process.

- When any solid or liquid is heated, the heat absorbed can be stored if the hot material is well insulated but the heat is always lost in the end. Domestic solar hot water panels can be used to heat water during the day so that hot water and some space heating are available at night.

- On a large scale, heat at a solar farm can be stored during the day by heating molten salts or solid pebbles, again with good insulation. The heat can then be used to make steam and generate electricity during the night. This can cope with daily variations but would not solve the problem of seasonal changes when moving into polar regions.

- Biofuels, including algal fuels, and synthetic fuels made from hydrogen and CO_2 extracted from the atmosphere can be readily stored and transported.

- Absorption of hydrogen on suitable pellets may become a significant means of storing and transporting hydrogen.

Storage can help with daily variations in supply but only pumped storage, biofuels or synthetic fuels can go any way towards helping with seasonal fluctuations in the supply of energy.

Scenarios For The Future

- Static Energy

Scenarios for the future supply of energy need to provide for everyone to get the energy needed when they need it. Electricity is the major type of energy and has to be distributed via a grid. Virtually every house, office, school, hospital, shop, factory and train line or tram system will need to be connected to the grid. Details of the grid will need to take into account the characteristics of individual countries and regions. Production in a given country will not necessarily match the needs in that country and the grid will have to cross many international boundaries. Politics and security of supply will have a serious impact on how any grid is designed and both must be taken into account.

Nuclear power is a possibility in any country and energy can be distributed via a local grid. Furthermore, subject to appropriate planning, nuclear power can be available when needed so the simplest solution might be for all our static energy to come from this single source. However, since known reserves of nuclear fuels are limited this cannot be considered as a real long-term solution. Furthermore safety and security are particularly important issues where nuclear power is concerned.

Geothermal power is also available as needed so could be distributed to local countries with a relatively small grid. Although large scale geothermal power is only available at present in certain countries, particularly those around the Pacific Rim, there is some availability on every continent.

Hydroelectricity is also available as needed so long as planning ensures that the reservoirs are not completely drained. Again, although limited to specific countries, every continent has some potential.

Wind and wave power vary without any consistent pattern but when the output is low in one place, it may well be high in another. Again, a grid linking countries on a regional basis is likely to provide a more continuous source but backup from hydro and nuclear will also be essential.

Solar energy creates the greatest distribution problem because it is subject to both daily and seasonal variations. It will probably be sensible to locate solar farms in or close to the tropics where output per hectare is potentially double that in more temperate regions and where seasonal differences are less. They can then be linked to grids which carry power north or south into the temperate areas. This, however, does not deal with daily fluctuations. To have solar electricity in London I would need to be connected to California to give me electricity in the evening and to Jakarta to meet my early morning needs. A better means of dealing with the daily cycle may be to store some of the solar energy as heat during the day and use this to generate electricity at night.

Tidal energy is also on a regular cycle but overall it is likely to be a small component of total energy supply and there is no immediate way of compensating for the daily or monthly cycle.

As well as electricity from the grid, there is also the possibility of capturing energy on a small or domestic scale. In the future, I envisage every household and many other buildings having their own energy harvesting systems. This will consist of a mix of solar PV, solar heat and geothermal surface heat. Details of the mix will depend on location, needs and latitude. In rural areas, a substantial area of panels or ground source collectors may be possible and some people may overall be net exporters of energy. In urban areas, the possibilities are more limited but each building will make a contribution.

In addition, almost every building will be connected to the grid. Each grid will need to be considerably larger than national and can probably best be described as regional. Once electricity is in the system it is slightly artificial to attribute it to a particular source but doing so illustrates some of the principles.

First of all the grid will be supplied with electricity from solar PV sources in the tropics with the daily variations partly smoothed by storage of solar heat. In the same way, any tidally generated electricity available will be fed into the system without any possibility of smoothing the fluctuations.

Next, energy from irregular sources such a wind will be added to the supply. At this point, the available supply of electricity would be variable with random, weather-related fluctuations on top of daily and seasonal ones. Next, any available geothermal electricity will be fed into the system as required and finally supply will be matched with demand by using locally available hydroelectricity or nuclear power which can be adjusted as required with appropriate forecasts and planning.

Details of the power sources used will be different for every grid system and will fluctuate with time. The size of a grid system has to be such that everyone connected to it has a reliable source of electricity available 24/7. And remember that "reliable" includes both technical reliability and political security.

In this way, almost every location will have enough electricity and heat to meet their needs all the time. There will be a few remote locations which cannot be connected to a grid. These can have local solar PV systems which will provide power during the day as well as charging batteries to provide power during the night. With any luck, batteries will in the future be considerably more efficient than those which are available today. An alternative for these off-grid locations is to use biofuels or synthetic fuels to run a local generator.

- Transport

Part of transport needs will be powered by electricity from the grid system described above. The rest of it requires portable energy which comes, in the main, from biofuels. Even with current methods the World can probably produce an adequate supply of biofuels while still growing enough food for everyone. With improvements in cultivation we should have more than enough of both. However, synthetic fuels produced from hydrogen and CO_2 could also become a significant source.

There will also be some savings in demand for biofuels by increased use of batteries in cars. These batteries will be recharged through use of electricity from the grid. If, in the future, lighter, longer lasting and more efficient batteries are developed these may well make a significant contribution to our transport needs.

Hydrogen is sometimes trumpeted as a renewable, carbon neutral fuel. At present it is neither because electricity is used in its production and this is often generated by burning fossil fuels. This situation will change in the future as more electricity is generated from sunlight or waves etc. Furthermore, in the future, hydrogen could be used as a portable fuel. Carrying cylinders of high pressure hydrogen in the boot of your car might not seem such a good idea but absorption onto solid pellets is a possibility and production of synthetic fuels may become an option. There is also a possibility that electric cars could run on electricity generated by hydrogen fuel cells. Fuel cells have the ability to convert the "heat" from a chemical reaction directly into electrical energy with a high level of efficiency. These have been about to come onto the market for over fifty years but at last they are now being offered to the public though they are still very expensive. Perhaps a crucial discovery will make them more economic in the near future.

A Final Conclusion

World demand for energy in 2150 can be met from renewable, carbon neutral sources but we have to start implementing relevant schemes very quickly. To keep the global temperature rise below a further 1°C, we need, by 2030, to reduce fossil fuel consumption by 50% compared to present levels. By 2050 fossil fuel consumption must be down by 95% and it must be totally eliminated by 2075. We have to accelerate development of renewable energy schemes starting now. In the last thirty years we have increased production of renewable energy by 50%. In the next thirty years we need to increase the quantity of renewables available by a further factor of three to limit temperature rise to a further 2°C or by a factor of six to limit it to only 1°C. To achieve the latter we need to develop renewables 12 times faster in the next 35 years than we have done in the last 35 years. It will be difficult to do this but we really must try.

Future plans must take into account security of supply and this inevitably has substantial political implications.

Chapter 11

Progress So Far

For many years, a substantial number of scientists have believed that man-made Climate Change is a reality and, although it is not absolutely certain, the overwhelming probability, despite the sceptics, is such that we should act on the assumption that Global Warming is real.

There is now a crucial need for international agreement and for global cooperation. We must agree targets for limiting overall growth in energy demand as well as making availability of energy in every country and region more equal. Furthermore, we need a schedule for very rapidly replacing fossil fuels with renewables, which is consistent with the overall targets defined in Chapter 9 and we need a means of monitoring performance and forcing countries to meet their targets. In the past, there have been other problems which, like this one, have needed global agreement to provide solutions. What we have done to solve these gives some clues as to how we might limit man-made Climate Change?

Self Interest Is The Driver

International agreements frequently involve one group getting together to protect themselves, physically or economically, from another group. Some agreements, however, have involved most countries in the World and, with varying degrees of success, have sought to improve overall welfare. The Nuclear Non-Proliferation Treaty was designed to limit the spread of nuclear weapons. 189 countries are party to the treaty, five of which have nuclear weapons but who are supposed to be disarming. Three other countries, India, Israel and Pakistan are not party to the treaty but do have nuclear weapons. It could be argued that the treaty has had little real impact and all countries have just done what they see as in their own best interests by joining, refusing to join or withdrawing when it suits them.

In 1946, the International Whaling Convention was set up to protect the whale population and the convention now has 59 signatories including Japan. In 1982, a moratorium was placed on the hunting of whales but the

Japanese go on catching them in the pretence that they are undertaking scientific research. There are similar problems with stocks of many other fish throughout the World's oceans. Countries usually consider their own short-term national benefits without considering the longer term adverse consequences for the World as a whole.

In the past, we have had only limited success in reaching international agreement over long-term issues. If we are to succeed in getting effective action to prevent Global Warming, we have to look at the interests of our successors across the whole world over the next few hundred years and we have to recognise that this may put some limitations on what we ourselves can do today. In addition we must also to accept the need to put **global** interests above our own **national** interests.

A Success Story

The ozone in the upper layers of the atmosphere protects the Earth from some of the ultraviolet radiation coming from the Sun. In 1974, it was suggested that the leakage and release of chlorofluorocarbons (CFCs) and related compounds used in refrigeration and air conditioning systems was leading to depletion of the ozone layer as the gases diffused slowly into the upper atmosphere. In 1987 the Montreal Protocol was agreed to phase out the use of these compounds and this has since been ratified by all UN members. As has recently been confirmed the rate of depletion of the ozone layer has been halted solely as a result of this international agreement. Because of almost universal international cooperation, this treaty has been successful in combating a modest threat. Perhaps this treaty was only possible because there were alternatives to CFCs which cost very little more – i.e. meeting the treaty cost individual countries virtually nothing. There have recently been suggestions that some of the alternatives to CFCs, namely hydrofluorocarbons (HFCs) and hydrochlorofluorocarbons (HCFCs) can have a similar though less serious effect so we still have to keep watching.

Can we draw up another international treaty to cover the eventual elimination of the use of fossil fuels and their replacement with energy from renewables? This will be much more complicated and may well be seen as having short-term disadvantages for some of us, particularly in Developed Countries, but to be successful we must all participate. The proposal at the 2014 UN Climate Change Summit to develop a comprehensive global strategy for signature at the talks in Paris in 2015 is exactly what is needed if only it can be achieved.

UNFCCC

At the "Earth Summit" in Rio de Janeiro in 1992, an international environmental treaty was drawn up. It came into force in 1994 and it now has 196 signatories or "parties" including all the members of the United Nations. The objective defined in the treaty, the United Nations Framework Convention on Climate Change (UNFCCC), "is to stabilise greenhouse gas concentrations in the atmosphere at a level that will prevent dangerous anthropogenic interference with the climate".

Since 1995 there has been an annual Conference of the Parties, or COP, at which additions have been made to the original terms of the treaty. The venues for the COPs from 1995 to 2015 are shown in the box below.

Where the COPs have been held since 1995		
COP1 1995 Bonn	COP8 2002 New Delhi	COP15 2009 Copenhagen
COP2 1996 Geneva	COP9 2003 Milan	COP16 2010 Cancun
COP3 1997 Kyoto	COP10 2004 Buenos Aires	COP17 2011 Durban
COP4 1998 Buenos Aires	COP11 2005 Montreal	COP18 2012 Doha
COP5 1999 Bonn	COP12 2006 Nairobi	COP19 2013 Warsaw
COP6 2000 The Hague	COP13 2007 Bali	COP20 2014 Lima
COP7 2001 Bonn	COP14 2008 Poznan	COP21 2015 Paris

The Kyoto Protocol

The initial convention was a statement of intent. It contained no specific limits or any enforcement mechanism. At COP3 in Japan in 1997 the treaty evolved into the Kyoto Protocol, by far the best known international agreement concerning Climate Change. The Protocol included targets for the reduction, by 2012, of GHG emissions by Developed countries relative to their emissions in 1990. The Protocol was, however, light on targets and light on methods of enforcement.

The parties to the Convention (see Appendix C) are divided into a three groups:

- Annex I includes 40 industrialized countries including 17 EITs (Economies in Transition = Eastern Europe) plus the European Union.
- Annex II, a subset of Annex I, 23 Developed Countries and the EU.
- The remaining 156 parties are Developing Countries or are very small.

- Targets And Performance

The aim of the Kyoto Protocol was to put some targets into the Framework Convention. The Protocol could not become effective until it was ratified by at least 55 signatories to UNFCCC and by enough of the Annex I countries to account for 55% of the total 1990 emissions of this group. The first condition was met in 2002. The second condition was met in 2004 when Russia eventually joined in and the protocol was ratified in 2005. It has now been ratified by 192 countries but the USA, whose emissions account for over a third of the total from all Annex I countries, have still not ratified it.

The next table shows a summary of data for the various groups of countries which have ratified the protocol and for the USA. Further details are given in Appendix C.

Groups of countries relating to UNFCCC and to the Kyoto Protocol with data on their CO_2e emissions						
Country	No.	Total MT CO_2e		Change in CO_2e		T CO_2e /Cap
		1990	2012	90-12	Target	
Annex II	23	12,902	12,891	0%	-6%	14.1
EIT	14	5,971	3,688	-38%	-2%	12.2
Other Annex I	3	189	440	133%		6.0
Total Annex I	40	19,062	17091	-11%	-6%	13.2
Developing World	147	14,938	30,981	107%	-	5.9
World Total	187	34,000	48,000	41%	-	7.4
EU-25	25	5,771	4,519	-22%	-7%	9.0
EU-15	15	4,275	3,638	-15%	-8%	9.6

Each row shows the total emissions of carbon dioxide equivalents[a] (CO_2e) in 1990 based on data published by UNFCCC, together with the actual emissions measured in 2012. The table also shows the actual percentage change from 1990 to 2012 together with the targets set at Kyoto or as subsequently updated.

The base year for the reduction targets is 1990 but note that targets were only set for the Developed world. The overall target set for the original 15 EU countries was an 8% reduction by 2012 although they subsequently

---

[a] CO_2e is the amount of CO_2 which would have the same GHG effect as all the GHGs present allowing for the fact that the effect of some them is greater than that of CO_2 at the same concentration.

agreed between themselves to a redistribution of the target. The final column shows the actual per capita emissions in 2012.

The allocation of targets, as shown in Appendix C does not appear to follow any obvious pattern. No correction is made for the fact that some of the emissions in one country may have been generated to make products which are consumed in another - it could be argued that such emissions should be the responsibility of the consuming rather than the producing country. A further limitation is that no figures for international air traffic or shipping are included.

The Impact Of Kyoto

The first chart in Appendix C shows how things had changed by 2012. The countries are listed in descending order of the percentage increase in their emission of carbon dioxide as shown by the grey bars. The targets set by Kyoto are shown by the black bars.

The changes range from an increase of over 100% at the top of the chart to a reduction of more than 50% at the bottom. When the grey bar for a country is to the left of the black bar its target has already been exceeded. Remember the Annex I countries originally had an obligation to meet their targets by 2012. Unfortunately, the USA still refuses to ratify the protocol because of concern about the impact on its own economy but some Democratic politicians are now beginning the recognise the problem.

Fourteen countries actually increased their emissions despite the fact that five of them had targets requiring a decrease. At the other end of the scale are twelve of the thirteen EIT countries. These have all achieved very considerable reductions in emissions. This is a reflection of the initial high levels resulting from coal-hungry industrialisation during the communist period. When this ended there were widespread opportunities for them to improve efficiency and they have done so.

In the middle of the chart are the main Developed Countries. All except Sweden had negative targets. Many of them met their targets by 2012 but some, among them the USA and Japan, actually increased their emissions.

Annex II countries which should be leading the field actually increased their emissions by 1% despite having a target for a reduction of 6%. Overall, the original 15 EU countries, all of whom are in Annex II, reduced their emissions by 14% well above the 2012 target of 8%. A number of these EU 15 countries (France, Belgium, Sweden, UK and Germany) comfortably met their targets but those in Southern Europe did not. The real problem, however, arises from the sharp increase in other countries, particularly in the USA, up by 6%.

It is generally accepted that in order for the economies of the Developing World to catch up with the Developed World, their emissions are going to increase substantially. Between 1990 and 2012, emissions in the Developing World increased by over 100% leading to an overall increase of more than 40% in total World emissions. If there had been no Kyoto Protocol and the emissions from Annex I countries had remained unchanged the overall increase would have been 44%. The effect of the Protocol appears to have been to reduce this to 40% - not a massive change!

However, in the absence of the Protocol, emissions from Annex I countries might actually have increased. If this were true then the impact of Kyoto could be greater than suggested above. **It is, nonetheless, indisputable that in the very near future very much greater savings in emissions will be needed.**

- Per Capita Emissions

The second chart in Appendix C shows per capita emissions for Annex I countries and for other groups of countries. There are huge differences. Luxembourg is near the top of the list but this is artificial because people nip across the border from adjacent countries to buy cheap petrol. The high figures for other top countries to some extent reflect their geography - because of long distances, people travel more.

Developing Countries will undoubtedly increase their emissions in the immediate future. Emissions in China increased by over 200% between 1992 and 2013 and those in India doubled over the same period. However, per capita emissions in the USA are almost five times the current level for China and if exports were taken into account, the net result for China would be even lower.

The overall target set for Annex I countries in the Kyoto Protocol was a reduction of 6% in emissions over 22 years. This is a very modest target and only applied to the Developed World. In practice the reduction was 10%. Much of the reduction is the result of one-off changes in the EITs while a number of other countries have actually increased their emissions. If we are to meet the essential overall targets for the future, as discussed elsewhere, very much more positive action will be needed.

After Kyoto

As the deadline for meeting the Kyoto targets approached attempts were made to extend the figures into the future. The meeting in Copenhagen in November 2009 was COP15 and its objective was to update the Kyoto Protocol to arrive at a new set of targets when Kyoto expired at the end of 2012. At the time the plan was for the new Protocol to be finalised during COP16 which was held in Cancun at the end of 2010.

The Copenhagen meeting was indecisive and received very negative press. At the end of the conference the Copenhagen Accord was agreed. Some of the main points in the accord are shown below. The points are very general and do not lead to positive actions. This point is emphasised by the items not included, which are shown in the second box.

Targets from the Copenhagen Accord

- Aspirational 2ºC above pre-industrial level target for global temperature rise – this is equivalent to 1ºC above the current level.
- Emissions "to peak as soon as possible".
- Pledged quantified economy-wide emissions targets for 2020 by Developed Countries (yet to be filled in), to be reviewed every 2 years.
- Pledged nationally appropriate mitigation actions of Developing Countries (yet to be filled in), to be reviewed every 2 years.
- International monitoring, reporting and verifying for Developed Countries.
- Domestic emissions must be measurable, reportable and verifiable and there will be "international consultations and analysis" for Developing Countries.
- US$30 billion aid for 2010-2012 to Developing Countries.
- US$100 billion yearly by 2020, (via the Green Climate Fund) to assist Developing Countries to adapt to Climate Change, reduce deforestation, and de-carbonize their development.
- North-South transfer of technology.

After the closing of the conference, the UNFCCC received national pledges to cut, or at least limit, emissions from 75 countries. Between them, these 75 countries account for 80% of total global emissions. There is, however, no clarity on how the various "decisions" in the Accord were to be taken forward.

What's missing from the Copenhagen Accord

- No medium term emission goals, no practical pathway to the 2°C target.
- No commitment to halving global emissions by 2050 as is necessary to meet the 2°C target.
- No agreement on specific emission reduction commitments.
- No deadline to complete a legally binding instrument.
- No requirement to review the agreement in the light of the latest science.
- No commitment to a compliance mechanism.
- No financial commitment for 2015-2020.
- No commitment that long term (post 2020) public finance for Developing Countries will be additional to existing development assistance.

The Executive Secretary of UNFCCC, Yvo de Boer, is on record as saying in March 2010 that "while the pledges on the table are an important step towards the objective of limiting the growth of emissions, they will not, of themselves suffice to limit Global Warming to 2°C above preindustrial levels (i.e. 1°C above the current level). The Climate Conference at the end of this year in Mexico (i.e. in Cancun in 2010) therefore needs to put in place effective cooperative mechanisms capable of bringing about acceleration of national and international action to limit the growth of emissions and to prepare for the inevitable impacts of Climate Change".

The mechanisms de Boer had said were needed were by no means fully put in place in Cancun when the conference was held. There was no success in agreeing future targets and it was recognised that revised figures were not going to be agreed by 2012 - the date was moved forward to 2015.

One positive result of COP16 in Cancun was establishment of the Green Climate Fund. This is a UNFCCC fund set up as a means of transferring money from Developed countries to Developing ones to help them mitigate the impact of climate change. When first established it had an unofficial goal of having $100bn available each year by 2020. To date a total of just over $10bn has been committed to the fund including $3bn from USA and approximately $1bn each from France, Germany, Japan and UK with smaller contributions from another twenty countries. There is, however, still a very long way to go to reach the 2020 target.

There was little further progress in setting targets at the next two COPs in Durban and Doha but at COP19 in Warsaw in 2013 it was agreed that outline targets would be drafted at COP20 in Lima, Peru in 2014 and that these would be finalised at COP21 in Paris in December 2015.

Despite the lack of agreement on specific targets a number of general principles have evolved since the original establishment of the UNFCCC in the early 1990s. Current commitments of all signatories to the convention, after taking into account the discussions in Warsaw, are shown in the box below.

Commitments of all UNFCCC signatories after COP19

- publish and update data on net emissions of GHGs.
- formulate plans for reduction of GHG emissions.
- cooperate in development and transfer of relevant technology.
- promote sustainable management and enhancement of relevant sinks.
- cooperate in preparing for adaptation to the impact of Climate Change.
- take Climate Change into account in all planning of social, economic and environmental policies.
- promote and cooperate in scientific and other research into further understanding and mitigation of Climate Change.
- cooperate in the exchange of such information.
- promote education and understanding of Climate Change matters.
- communicate all relevant information to the COPs.

Additional commitments for Annex I and Annex II parties are shown in the next box. These objectives are all entirely worthy and commendable but they are very generalised, they include no specific targets and they completely lack any teeth.

Additional commitments for all Annex I countries after COP19

- adopt national policies to mitigate anthropogenic emission of GHGs and enhance sinks to demonstrate that Developed Countries are taking a lead in modifying longer term trends in anthropogenic emissions.
- publish all plans and regularly update projections of net emissions of GHGs with the aim of reducing net emissions back to their 1990 levels.
- the above should be based on the best scientific information available.
- furthermore the above commitments will be regularly reviewed and revised as necessary.
- cooperate on the above with other parties and review their own policies with respect to activities which increase emissions.
- review the countries included on the Annex I and Annex II lists.
- any country not in Annex I may agree at any time to abide by these conditions.

Further obligations were placed on Annex II countries to help with the financing of emission control in Developing Countries. These again are very worthy but, despite the Green Climate Fund, it is very difficult to know to what extent they have been, or will be, implemented. Furthermore, if a Developed Country finances emission reduction in a Developing Country the savings may be treated as part of the emission reductions of the donor country.

Additional commitments for all Annex II countries after COP19

- provide new and additional financial resources to meet costs incurred by Developing Countries in meeting their obligations as defined above.
- assist particularly vulnerable Developing Countries in adapting to the adverse effects of Climate Change and in meeting the costs.
- take all practicable steps to facilitate and finance the adoption of appropriate technology in Developing Countries.

COP20 in Lima almost ended without any agreement at all but after continuing for an extra two days their conclusions were summarised in a "Call for Climate Action". All parties should submit their contributions for inclusions in the agreement to be finalised in Paris in 2015. These Intended Nationally Determined Contributions (INDCs) will form the foundation for climate action after 2020 when the new agreement is set to come into effect. This was the key outcome of the discussions which sadly, once again, postpones all really significant action.

The Call for Climate Action includes a number of detailed points such as adding the subject of climate change awareness to school curricula and to national development plans as well as looking at the impact of climate change on human migration and displacement. Certain countries also submitted data on how GHG emissions can be reduced in the forestry sector. Developing countries are concerned that steps to combat climate change will seriously impact on their economic growth.

Overall there is grave concern that there is still a significant gap between existing pledges and the reductions in emissions which are really needed.

In the future there has to be much more commitment and it will have to be recognised that there will be costs, at least in the short-term, associated with taking the necessary environmental steps. The constant procrastination has to come to an end but, as we will discuss in Chapter 12, getting 200 different parties to reach an agreement is probably not feasible. Another way of reaching agreement is needed.

Chapter 12

What We Must Do In The Future

The majority of scientists believe that Climate Change is, in part, man-made and that because of the potential seriousness of the consequences we should take steps to reduce our emissions of GHGs and we need to begin **NOW**.

In this book I have presented estimates of the amount of energy the World will need up to 2150 and how this energy can be supplied while keeping the global temperature within a reasonable limit. This can be done by improving the efficiency with which we use energy and by developing renewable, carbon neutral, sources.

The potential risk from Global Warming has been recognised for at least 25 years and some efforts have been made to introduce international policies to limit the temperature rise, largely through the Kyoto Protocol. To date these efforts have had only a small effect as discussed in the previous chapter.

In the next section I have set out a list of key ideas which have to be taken into consideration if we are to develop a strategy which will help to mitigate the impact of Climate Change on the lives of our children, grandchildren and great grandchildren. The background to many of the points listed has been discussed earlier but there are some areas which need additional comment and these are covered later in this chapter.

The Key Ideas

Apart from scientists, most political leaders and many individuals recognise that Global Warming is an issue which needs to be addressed. They also recognise that, to deal with it, renewable energy will have to be brought widely into use and very quickly. The additional fact that fossil fuels are finite is seldom mentioned. In order to ensure sustainable and equitable availability of energy for the foreseeable future a number of ideas have to be taken on board.

The key ideas are as follows:

a) We have to accept that Global Warming is a fact and that the activities of Mankind are one of the major causes. The risks are such that we should take steps to minimise "anthropogenic" Climate Change and we need to begin **NOW**.

b) Extreme poverty undoubtedly leads to unhappiness but, above a fairly low level of wealth, happiness and well-being do not necessarily continue to increase as we get richer. We have to stop chasing eternal economic growth.

c) The preceding point applies particularly to the Developed World. If we continue our obsessive pursuit of economic growth, we will very rapidly run out of a variety of other resources apart from energy.

d) Wealth, and as a consequence energy consumption, is very unequally distributed around the globe. We need to accept that a more equal distribution of these is both just and inevitable and we need to take steps to reduce the enormous disparities both within our own countries and across international boundaries.

e) Total consumption of energy needs to be kept within manageable limits and by the middle of this century most of World energy must come from renewable sources. By the end of the century, the use of fossil fuels, as a source of energy, must have been totally eliminated.

f) One of the factors leading to increased demand for energy has been population growth. This may be levelling off but it is an issue which must be kept in mind when developing plans for the future and all possible efforts should be made to ensure that the population levels off at about 10 billion.

g) Many people in the Developed World recognise the need to use energy efficiently but the message needs to be more widely accepted throughout the World. Energy efficiency should be pursued at all levels.

h) The cost of energy is likely to rise as the proportion of renewables increases but then, despite the recent fall in the price of oil, the long term cost of fossil fuels will also increase as their availability becomes restricted. Increased costs and additional taxation may have to be accepted.

i) There will be costs associated with developing renewable sources and a system will be needed so that rich countries give financial and technical support to the poorer nations. This will result in developments taking place which will ultimately benefit us all.

j) Use of renewables sometimes has local disadvantages as well as global benefits. We must assess projects on the overall balance of their costs and benefits to the World as a whole. Real objections must be taken seriously but Nimbyism has to be quashed!

k) A global plan has to be agreed setting targets for total energy consumption and the proportion to be derived from renewables. Each country will have its own targets and a schedule must be designed to lead eventually to more equitable availability and consumption of energy. The plan must be flexible and it will have to evolve to take advantage of continuing technological developments.

l) A system for monitoring performance in each country will be required. A method for encouraging each country to meet its targets will also be needed. This might involve a bonus for good performance and/or a penalty for failing to meet targets.

m) Many countries will not be able to supply, from within their own boundaries, all their energy needs at all times. A system allowing the transfer of energy across international boundaries will be required. This must provide security of supply for every country and measures will be needed to minimise the opportunities for one country to blackmail another.

The discussion below covers these ideas in varying levels of detail where they have not been covered in earlier chapters. There is not yet a complete solution to all the questions, some of which will remain unanswered for some time to come. Many solutions will only be reached after years of discussion at local, national and international levels and ideas will change as further developments emerge. Widespread discussion of ideas, which has already begun, needs to expand. Some partial solutions need to be put into effect as soon as possible, though with the realisation that many of the details will continue to evolve.

Growth In GDP

We live in a World where economics has been obsessed for many years with growth in our wealth, usually measured as GDP. The recent economic crashes and our eventual emergence from them can all be measured by plotting changes in GPD. Furthermore the difference between countries is frequently illustrated by quoting the difference in their per capita GPD.

The average global GDP per capita in 2013 was $13,000 per year but in the USA was $53,000. In sub-Saharan Africa it was about $700 and it fell to only $550 in the Central African Republic. Over the last century, per capita GDP in the USA, after adjusting for inflation, has increased by a factor of about 12 from about $4,500 to the current level. Meanwhile the population has risen from 75 million to about 300 million. Total GDP for the USA thus rose by a factor of more than 50 during the twentieth century.

If per capita GPD in the USA increases at only 1% per annum it will still lead to an increase by a further factor of about 2.3 by 2100. Now imagine that the GDP in other countries grows at a higher rate so that by 2100 the per capita GDP in every country matches that in the USA. Meanwhile, the World population will almost certainly be at about 10 billion, an increase of over 30% above the current level, and it could go higher.

Combining these three factors would lead to an increase in total World GDP by a factor of sixteen by the end of this century compared to the current level. Continuing for another century with annual GDP growing at 1% per year for everyone, but with a stable population would lead to a global GDP by the year 2200 that would be forty times higher than the present level. Along with this increase, there will be a similar rise in consumption of most raw materials, including energy. It is improbable that every country will reach the level of the USA and increased recycling and more efficient use of energy will, to an extent, moderate demand for resources. Nonetheless, the calculation illustrates the dire consequences of our obsessive search for growth. There are simply not enough resources to support everyone along this road.

There is a bonus to all this. If we decide to consume less then we may not have to work as much. If, in the future, productivity increases further then perhaps we can cut to a three-day working week. The rest of the time, we can spend doing the things we enjoy most.

The effect of the current economic recession is difficult to foresee. However, we appear to be emerging from it and it could, perhaps, lead to the realisation among the wealthier countries that continued growth is no longer necessary.

What Is Happiness?

Since our continual demand for economic growth seems to be fuelled by a search for greater happiness it is worth asking at this stage "what is happiness?" If I am permanently hungry and my family is perpetually short of food, it would be reasonable to describe myself as unhappy. If I discover how to increase my PDP (personal domestic product) by growing wheat, so that I can bake enough bread to ward of the pangs of hunger, I will become dramatically happier. If I continue to develop my skills so that I have more variety of food, I will become somewhat more happy but perhaps only a little. The big change will already have occurred when I moved from hunger to sufficiency.

There have been a number of studies showing that when GDP is very low "happiness" itself is also low and that happiness does rise with increase in income. But this interdependence only applies at the bottom of the scale. At a modest income, happiness reaches a "normal" level and a further increase in income does not, in general, lead to greater happiness. The happiness of an individual is much more dependent on individual characteristics and circumstances in their life well beyond income.

The level of happiness appears to be strongly related to the evenness with which income is distributed across society. The Gini Index is the ratio of the income of the wealthiest 20% of the population of a given country divided by that of the poorest 20%. Scandinavian countries, with a Gini Index of 4 are at the top of the happiness index. The USA with an Index of 10 is way down the list.

Based solely on per capita GPD, the USA lies fifth in the World, behind Qatar, Luxembourg, Norway and Singapore. The United Nations Human Development Index (HDI) is a measure of development which takes into account, not only GDP, but also life expectancy and education. On this basis, the top of the list is Norway with the USA down at thirteenth place while the UK is at 21. Bottom of the list is the Republic of Niger. The New Economic Foundation has developed the "Happy Planet Index" which combines the HDI with a measure of the long term sustainability of the lifestyle in each country. On this basis, Costa Rica comes out top with the UK down at 74 and the USA at 114. These alternative scales are not perfect but they certainly illustrate other points of view and the USA clearly has a lifestyle which could not be sustainable both long term and globally.

I first drafted this section while staying at a monastery in the South of France. The monks who live there enjoy a remarkable level of happiness while consuming a very modest amount of the World's resources.

The future demand for energy, as estimated for the Preferred Scenario in Chapter 9, is based on the convergence of all countries on a per capita consumption of energy close to the current level in Europe. This implies that per capita GDP also levels of at the current European level and the arguments above suggest that this will not in fact impact on the overall happiness of the World population. The estimated demand for energy is a realistic target although it may be somewhat too high for a sustainable "Happy Planet".

Conflict Of Interest

Development of production and distribution facilities for both conventional and renewable energy frequently have an impact on the local environment. Overhead power lines disfigure the landscape and some people argue that living next to them creates a health hazard. Wind farms are often considered ugly and noisy. Solar panels may destroy the charm of a Georgian roof. What happens if terrorists attack a nuclear power plant and in any case can nuclear waste be disposed of safely?

Whenever a new development is being considered there will be a group of people who object. Often it is not that they object to wind farms per se, just that they don't want one where they can see or hear it – this truly is Nimbyism.

There is a continuing dilemma in balancing the benefits of the World at large against real or imagined disadvantages of a much smaller number of individuals. In China, the Three Gorges hydroelectric project will eventually have a generating capacity equivalent to about a quarter of the total UK capacity. The project will also improve navigation for 10,000 tonne barges along 660 km of waterway. However, construction of the project will involve relocation of up to 2 million people. Was it right to go ahead with this project?

There was a proposal for a small wind farm in the UK, in Lancashire. Locals were being encouraged to object because of its impact on the beauty of the landscape, on nearby homes and listed buildings and its effect on wildlife and recreational use of the land. Were all the objections real or were some of them blown out of proportion or even imagined?

What is the right balance between the benefits of the many against disadvantage to the few? Although the latter should not be ignored, the development of a sustainable energy policy is crucial to the World. There will undoubtedly be many contentious issues but decisions have to take into account the global benefit. We shall sometimes have to override the interests of the few and we should not automatically judge in favour of the rich and powerful, whether they be individuals or nations.

Incentives And Penalties

Carrots are usually more effective than sticks so any agreement should, as far as possible, concentrate on rewards for countries meeting their targets rather than on penalties for those who do not. It may, however, be difficult to avoid penalties altogether.

The most effective driver is always price. As technology develops renewables will become cheaper and at the same time fossil fuels will become scarcer and more expensive. This will be the ultimate driver but on its own is unlikely to bring results as quickly as needed. A tax on fossil fuels with the proceeds used to subsidise renewables may be a solution. The tax could be collected as the fuel is produced but it may be more effective if it is collected where the fuel is used. An electricity company would pay tax on the gas for its generators or drivers would pay it on the fuel in their tanks. Despite cries of horror something along these lines has to be done. It will give us each an incentive to use less energy and encourage the development of renewables. Taxation can be varied depending on the application and it should extend to aviation fuel which is now largely exempt from tax.

Taxation is usually looked upon in a negative light. However, collecting a tax generates funds which can be applied to some other activity. In this case, some of the tax collected will be used to subsidise development of renewables but it can be used to pay for public services or to allow a reduction of other taxes. In this case, the overall objective of the taxation is not to generate revenue but to redirect our expenditure.

Fuel prices vary considerably from one country to another and there needs to be some mechanism for reducing these differences. In Europe, the price of gasoline varies to some extent over time but in the USA the price is about 40% lower. The low price is, of course, one of the reasons why energy consumption in the USA is so high and why there are so many gas-guzzlers on the roads. It will, however, not be easy to get the USA electorate to accept a major increase in gasoline prices.

This taxation method, however, poses some problems particularly for the countries and companies exporting fossil fuels. Since the aim is to eliminate the use of fossil fuels altogether, it will also eliminate the income of the producers. For some countries this is a very high proportion of their GDP. A solution to this would be for at least part of the tax collected to be put into an "international fund" which would eventually be redistributed to the countries in greatest need.

Countries such as Saudi Arabia, Qatar or Kuwait have substantial investments from past oil revenues and are already planning for the days when their fossil fuels run out. Other countries such as Uzbekistan have been earning from fossil fuels for a much shorter time and have not had much time to build up reserves.

As part of an international agreement, a huge extension of Kyoto, every country will be set a schedule for overall energy consumption and for replacement of fossil fuels with renewables so as to reduce CO_2 emissions. The schedules will vary from country to country depending on the starting point. The aim should be to move towards total elimination of emissions well before the end of this century and towards the same per capita energy consumption in every country by about 2200. Ideally, every country will participate in setting targets for its own economy and will ratify the agreement.

Each country will have its own strategy for meeting these targets but a leading component of all strategies may well be taxation on the use of fossil fuels and it is possible that a minimum level of taxation can be agreed between countries.

The plan for development of renewables will also vary from country to country. Some countries can have ample supplies of renewables to meet their own needs while others will be dependent on imports from elsewhere so that they can meet demand for energy when and where it is needed. This will necessitate a great deal of international cooperation with one country subsidising development of renewables in another and groups of countries cooperating in the construction of power distribution systems.

Agreement of schedules and targets will be a long process and many countries will have to be persuaded to let their own short-term interests take second place to the greater good.

The eight leading producers of GHGs and their contribution to the global total are as follows:

- China - 27%
- USA - 17%
- The EU - 11%
- India - 6%
- Russia - 5%
- Japan - 4%
- South Korea - 2%
- Canada - 2%

Together these eight players account for three quarters of total emissions. They will have to take a central role in all discussions and it will certainly be useful if the EU remains a single party within the negotiations. Widespread PR to increase awareness of the problem and the feasibility and consequences of different solution will be essential. Reaching agreement will be difficult but it **must be done**.

Let us assume that schedules and targets have been agreed and satisfactory methods for monitoring performance have also been agreed. What happens if a country fails to meet its targets? This may be because the country is not really trying or because the actions it has taken were not sufficient to meet the requirements or they were not implemented properly. The first step will be to look at the methods being adopted to meet the targets. Should fuel tax be increased? Should subsidies for renewables be increased? Rectifying deficiencies here may put the country back on course.

However, some countries may be unwilling to take all the steps necessary to meet their targets. After all, of the 39 countries in Annex I who have ratified the Kyoto Protocol (see Appendix C) and agreed to its very modest targets, only 18 have yet met their targets for 2012 and 20 don't look as if they will get there in the near future. The USA is far from meeting the overall reduction target of 6% set for Annex II countries and it still refuses to ratify the protocol.

What do we do with countries which refuse to take part in negotiations, to ratify the agreement or fail to meet targets and appear to be making no serious effort to do so? The first step is additional PR targeted to raise the awareness of the general population of that country. Even if this fails, military force is out of the question so the last resort is economic sanctions. This could involve banning or limiting trade with the offending country, limiting travel to or from the country or imposing taxes on all goods which are supplied to the country. Ultimately, economic pressures within the country may force them to take appropriate action. It is, however, essential to keep the eight leading players on board from the outset.

Security Of Supply

Every country will need a reliable supply of energy which will meet its needs round the clock and throughout the year despite daily and seasonal variations in demand. In the past, this has been relatively easy as fossil fuels can be stored and used as required. Furthermore, if the fuels are being imported then if one supplier goes out of action another can be used. The increasing use of natural gas, particularly when supplied by pipeline has given more prominence to the storage question.

Some renewable energy can be stored. Hydro and nuclear power can be drawn on as required so long as there is appropriate short-term planning. Biofuels and synthetic fuels can be stored and there are methods for storing solar power either as heat or by using pumped storage. Technology will almost certainly improve the storage options, however, a great deal of renewable energy will come from the direct use of solar or wind power which has not been stored. To have the solar and wind power available round the clock during every season will require a vast international grid allowing flow of electricity in either direction since both demand and source of supply will vary.

The construction of this international grid will involve the cooperation of a substantial number of countries. Depending on the time of day or the season, each country involved in the grid may be a supplier, a consumer or merely a transporter. A consumer is inevitably vulnerable to the deliberate actions of either the supplier or the transporter and is also vulnerable to technical problems anywhere along the route as well as to terrorism. However, if a grid is wide enough there will be alternative routes from supplier to consumer or a different supplier can be drawn on.

It will be important when planning the grid to take into account long-term security of supply allowing for both the political and technical factors.

A Global Plan

To limit Global Warming we need a plan to abolish the use of fossil fuels and to develop and distribute renewable energy so that in the end everyone on the planet has access to the energy they need to live in comfort. At the beginning of this chapter I listed some ideas which need to be considered in any global agreement. Here are some more concrete points which have to be agreed:

a) Agree that the eternal growth in GDP is no longer feasible once per capita levels in individual countries are approximately equal to current levels in Europe.

b) Agree a target for the maximum acceptable global temperature rise for the foreseeable future.

c) Agree the maximum per capita energy consumption on a global basis, irrespective of whether that energy comes from fossil fuels or renewables. No country should exceed this limit until other countries have caught up. Some countries will have to reduce their per capita consumption. To meet this condition will necessitate limiting, or even reducing, GDP in some countries.

d) Agree a schedule for changes in per capita energy consumption in each country until they converge on the agreed common value sometime in the next century.

e) Agree a schedule for the increase in global energy consumption over the rest of this century based on the changes in per capita consumption and likely changes in population.

f) Agree a schedule for the maximum level of CO_2 emissions permissible on a global basis each year for the next 80 years by which time the level must be virtually zero. This schedule must be planned to keep the temperature rise within the limit agreed under point b).

g) Combine conclusions from points a) to f) to estimate the rate at which renewable energy sources have to be developed. This will undoubtedly necessitate a very considerable acceleration of the current rate at which renewables are being introduced.

h) Develop a strategy for producing the required amount of renewable energy in the countries where it can most effectively be produced and at the same time take into account appropriate methods of distribution so that it is available where and when it is needed. In Chapter 10 I estimated that we need to developed renewables 12 times faster between now and 2050 than we have been doing since 1980.

i) Include in the production and distribution strategies alternative sources, storage options and distribution routes to ensure security and reliability of supply for all countries.

j) Agree on methods for monitoring of performance in each country.

k) Agree on sanctions for those who refuse to cooperate or to make appropriate efforts to meet the targets to which they have agreed.

Waking Up

Is global agreement possible? The answer is "yes" but only "sometimes". As discussed in Chapter 11, the release of CFCs and related compounds into the atmosphere was leading to depletion of the ozone layer. This was generally recognised in the late 1970s and the Montreal Protocol, enacted in 1989, has halted the continuing reduction of the ozone layer.

That international treaty has been successful but it was a relatively simple problem compared to Global Warming. The Montreal Protocol dealt with a specific problem to which there was a simple solution which cost little extra. Can we draw up an international treaty but this time covering the elimination of fossil fuels and their replacement with renewables? An attempt has already been made by the UNFCCC through the Kyoto Protocol but with only very limited success so far.

However, before international agreement can be reached each country involved has to agree within itself that it will participate. Politicians are often reluctant make proposals which involve short term costs even if there are long term benefits and this will certainly apply to the steps individual countries will have to take to mitigate Climate Change. The only way to get round this is to increase public awareness of the problems and solutions so that the voters put pressure on the politicians who commit themselves to appropriate actions, even when these involve short term cost, in order to attract more votes.

There is some awareness of the problems of Global Warming but the subject needs much more publicity so that individuals appreciate the problems and are prepared to accept the need to put up with costs and inconvenience now to make savings in the future, if not for themselves at least for their children. This book is a contribution to the necessary publicity but it will need a very substantial input from the media. Perhaps more importantly large corporations will have to put aside their short term interests and think more about the long term. None of this will be easy but it is no good arguing that it is impossible – **IT HAS TO BE DONE.**

The agreement needed is an extension by UNFCCC of the Kyoto Protocol although, admittedly, a very considerable extension. However, the organisation exists and it should be used.

Ideally, we need a global agreement in which every country participates. However, what we need in the immediate future is the cooperation of the leading polluters. The chart below emphasises who these are. Just seven countries plus the EU account for 74% of global emissions. So long as the EU can agree among themselves, this is a reasonably small group which has some prospect of reaching an appropriate solution.

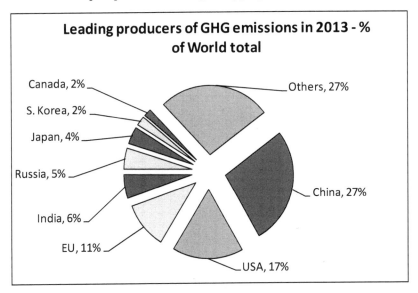

The next eight largest emitters, Iran, Mexico, South Africa, Saudi Arabia, Australia, Brazil, Indonesia and Poland, account for another 11% of emissions. These 16 key groups account for 85% of global emissions. The group includes representatives from all the continents as well as major Developing Countries.

Not represented are the smaller and poorer Developing Countries and care will need to be taken so as not to ignore their interests and in the end it will be important to bring on board the other 180 or so nations who make up the rest of the global community.

The plans will have to allow for all sorts of differences between individual countries. Not all the stages can be planned in detail at the outset.

Reasonably precise plans can, perhaps, be made for the next ten years but beyond that, they will have to be increasingly flexible and incorporate an element of uncertainty. Regular updating of targets will be needed.

The ultimate goal of this new agreement will be to keep the global temperature rise within an acceptable limit and at the same time to ensure that every country heads towards the same per capita energy consumption by 2200. Such a goal might be described as naïve or overly optimistic but unless some such goal is agreed, we will never get anywhere near it.

Of course it is easy to write down what ought to be in an agreement. In practice, it will be much more difficult to get the **UNSELFISH** cooperation of all the World's countries, however, for the long-term good of Mankind it has to be done.

On a global scale, the Kyoto Protocol may be judged to have had a small impact on emissions and what we need now is a very much more comprehensive treaty with teeth and a long-term set of targets. Drawing up the agreement will be a long and complex process and will require the good will of all concerned. The chances of getting most countries to join in will be greatly enhanced if the eight leading producers of GHGs all come on board at an early stage during the drafting of the agreement so that they are in a position to ratify it as soon as it is finalised. This, however, is by no means guaranteed – Russia was one of the last countries to ratify Kyoto and the USA still has not done so!

All the negotiators, whatever their nationality, need to be thinking about what is best for the World not just what is best for their own country. Each one **of us should be thinking along the same lines if we have the interest of our grandchildren and great-grandchildren at heart**.

We can take the steps needed to avoid unacceptable climate change even allowing for likely population growth but **WE MUST ALL WAKE UP NOW**. I have considerable doubts about everyone coming on board in time. Remember that in Chapter 10 I concluded that between now and 2050 we need to develop renewables 12 times faster than we have been doing recently. My major concern is that we will not take the necessary steps quickly enough. I am particularly concerned that the US will not fully commit themselves to seriously reducing their emissions. We must all put equality and global interests well ahead of our own purely national interests. Am I naive to think that this is even remotely possible?

Appendix A

Classification Of Countries

All countries have been classified by the United Nations as either Developed, NIC (Newly Industrialised Countries), Developing or LDC (Least Developed Countries). LDCs generally have a per capita income of less than $750 per year. The list contains 172 countries with a population of more than 50,000.

Developed Countries

Australia	Germany	Korea (South)	Sweden
Austria	Greece	Luxembourg	Switzerland
Belgium	Iceland	Netherlands	Turkey
Canada	Ireland	New Zealand	UK
Denmark	Israel	Norway	USA
Finland	Italy	Portugal	
France	Japan	Spain	

Newly Industrialised Countries (NICs)

Bahrain	Malaysia	Qatar	Thailand
China	Mexico	Saudi Arabia	Turkey
India	Oman	South Africa	UAE
Kuwait	Philippines	Taiwan	

Developing Countries

Albania	Czech Republic	Jordan	Paraguay
Algeria	Dominica	Kazakhstan	Peru
Argentina	Dominican	Kenya	Poland
Armenia	Republic	Korea (North)	Rep of Moldova
Azerbaijan	Ecuador	Uruguay	Romania
Barbados	Egypt	Uzbekistan	Russian Federation
Belarus	El Salvador	Venezuela	Serbia
Belize	Estonia	Vietnam	Singapore
Bolivia	Falklands	Kyrgyzstan	Slovakia
Bosnia	Gabon	Latvia	Slovenia
Brazil	Georgia	Lebanon	Sri Lanka
Brunei	Ghana	Libya	Suriname
Bulgaria	Greenland	Lithuania	Syria
Cameroon	Iraq	Mauritius	Tajikistan
Chile	Grenada	Mongolia	Trinidad & Tobago
Colombia	Guatemala	Morocco	Tunisia
Congo	Guyana	New Caledonia	Turkmenistan
Costa Rica	Honduras	Nicaragua	Ukraine
Cote d'Ivoire	Hungary	Nigeria	Venezuela
Croatia	Indonesia	Pakistan	Vietnam
Cuba	Iran	Panama	Zimbabwe
Cyprus	Jamaica	Papua New Guinea	

155

Least Developed Countries

Afghanistan	Equatorial Guinea	Malawi	South Sudan
Angola	Eritrea	Mali	Solomon Islands
Bangladesh	Ethiopia	Mauritania	Somalia
Benin	Gambia	Mozambique	Togo
Bhutan	Guinea	Myanmar	Tanzania
Burkina Faso	Guineau Bissau	Nepal	Uganda
Burundi	Haiti	Niger	Vanuatu
Cambodia	Kiribati	Rwanda	Yemen
CAR	Laos	Samoa	Zambia
Chad	Liberia	Senegal	
Dem Rep Congo	Lesotho	Sierra Leone	
East Timor	Madagascar	Sudan	

The OECD (Organisation for Economic Cooperation and Development) has 30 countries as members. Of these countries, 25 are Developed Countries but Mexico and Turkey are classified as Newly Industrialised Countries while Czech Republic, Hungary, and Slovakia are classified as Developing Countries.

OECD

Australia	Germany	Luxembourg	Spain
Austria	Greece	Mexico	Sweden
Belgium	Hungary	Netherlands	Switzerland
Canada	Iceland	New Zealand	Turkey
Czech Rep	Ireland	Norway	UK
Denmark	Italy	Poland	USA
Finland	Japan	Portugal	
France	Korea (South)	Slovakia	

G8 consists of the eight most economically powerful countries. All, except the Russian Federation, are members of OECD.

G8

Canada	Germany	Japan	UK
France	Italy	Russian Fed	USA

G20 consists of G8 plus 2 other Developed Countries, 6 NICs and 3 Developing Countries plus the EU. This is the next level of economic power.

G20 = G8 + Plus

Argentina	China	Korea	South Africa
Australia	India	Mexico	Turkey
Brazil	Indonesia	Saudi Arabia	EU

Heavy Emitters

Among the Heavy Emitters the first group account for 74% of total emissions, the second group account for a further 11%.

Top 8

China	EU	India	Canada
USA	Russia	Japan	Korea (South)

Second 8

Iran	South Africa	Australia	Indonesia
Mexico	Saudi Arabia	Brazil	Ukraine

EUROPEAN UNION

EU 15 in 2004

Austria	France	Italy	Spain
Belgium	Germany	Luxembourg	Sweden
Denmark	Greece	Netherlands	UK
Finland	Ireland	Portugal	

Joined EU in 2004

Cyprus	Estonia	Lithuania	Slovakia
Czech	Hungary	Malta	Slovenia
Republic	Latvia	Poland	

Joined EU in 2007

Bulgaria	Romania

BASIC = 4 Newly Industrializing Countries

Brazil	India	South Africa	China

157

Appendix B

Acronyms

AGW	Anthropogenic Global Warming
BTOE	Billion Tonnes of Oil Equivalent
CCS	Carbon Capture and Storage
CFC	ChloroFluoroCarbon
CFL	Compact Fluorescent Light
CH_4	Methane
CO_2	Carbon Dioxide
CO_2e	Carbon Dioxide Equivalent
COP	Conference of the Parties (signatories of UNFCCC)
EITs	Economies in Transition - ex members of the communist bloc
EU	European Union
GDP	Gross Domestic Product
GHG	Greenhouse Gas
HCFC	HydroChloroFluorocarbon
HDI	Human Development Index
HFC	Hydro Fluorocarbon
IAEA	International Atomic Energy Association
IEA	International Energy Association
INDC	Intended Nationally Determined Contributions
IPCC	Intergovernmental Panel on Climate Change
kWh	kiloWatt hour
LDC	Least Developed Countries
LED	Light Emitting Diodes
LIA	Little Ice Age
MTOE	Million Tonnes of Oil Equivalent
MWP	Medieval Warm Period
NASA	National Aeronautics and Space Administration
NOAA	National Oceanographic and Atmospheric Administration
OECD	Organisation for Economic Cooperation and Development
ppm	parts per million

SI	Systeme International (official units)
TFR	Total Fertility Rate
TOE	Tonnes of Oil Equivalent
UN	United Nations
UNDP	United Nations Development Programme
UNFCCC	United Nations Framework Convention on Climate Change
WEC	World Energy Council

Annex I parties to the Kyoto Protocol

Country	MT CO2e		Change in CO2e		T CO2e
	1990	2012	90-12	Target	/Capita
Annex II Countries					
Australia	415	544	31%	8%	24.4
Austria	78	80	3%	-13%	9.5
Belgium	143	117	-18%	-8%	10.6
Canada	591	699	18%	-6%	20.4
Denmark	70	53	-24%	-21%	9.5
Finland	70	61	-13%	0%	11.3
France	560	496	-11%	0%	7.6
Germany	1,248	939	-25%	-21%	11.5
Greece	105	111	6%	25%	10.0
Iceland	4	4	26%	10%	15.1
Ireland	55	59	6%	13%	12.7
Italy	519	460	-11%	-7%	7.7
Japan	1,234	1,343	9%	-6%	10.5
Luxembourg	13	12	-8%	-28%	22.8
Netherlands	212	192	-10%	-6%	11.5
New Zealand	61	76	25%	0%	17.3
Norway	50	53	5%	1%	10.7
Portugal	61	69	13%	27%	6.5
Spain	284	341	20%	15%	7.3
Sweden	73	58	-21%	4%	6.1
Switzerland	53	51	-3%	-8%	6.5
UK	783	586	-25%	-13%	9.3
USA	6,220	6,488	4%		20.8
Economies in Transition (EITs)					
Belarus	139	79	-43%	-8%	8.3
Bulgaria	122	61	-50%	-8%	8.4
Croatia	32	26	31%	-5%	6.1
Estonia	196	131	-33%	-8%	12.5
Czech Rep	41	19	-53%	-8%	14.4
Hungary	114	62	-46%	-6%	6.1
Latvia	26	11	-58%	-8%	5.2
Lithuania	49	22	-56%	-8%	7.2
Poland	570	399	-30%	-6%	10.4
Romania	285	119	-58%	-8%	5.9
Russian Fed	3,363	2,295	-32%	0%	16.1
Slovakia	73	43	-42%	-8%	7.9
Slovenia	20	19	-6%	-8%	9.3
Ukraine	940	401	-57%	0%	8.8
Other Countries					
Liechenstein	0.23	0.23	-1%	-8%	6.3
Monaco	0.11	0.09	-15%	-8%	2.5
Turkey	188	440	133%		6.0
Total Annex II	**12,902**	**12,891**	**0%**	**-6%**	**14.1**
EIT	5,971	3,688	-38%	-2%	12.2
Other	189	440	133%		6.0
Total Annex I	**19,062**	**17,019**	**-11%**	**-6%**	**13.2**
Developing World	14,938	30,981	107%		5.9
World Total	**34,000**	**48,000**	**41%**		**7.4**
EU - 25	5,771	4,519	-22%	-7%	9.0
EU - 15	4,275	3,633	-15%	-8%	9.6
USA	6,220	6,488	4%	-8%	20.8
Annex I less US	12,842	10,531	-18%	-4%	10.8

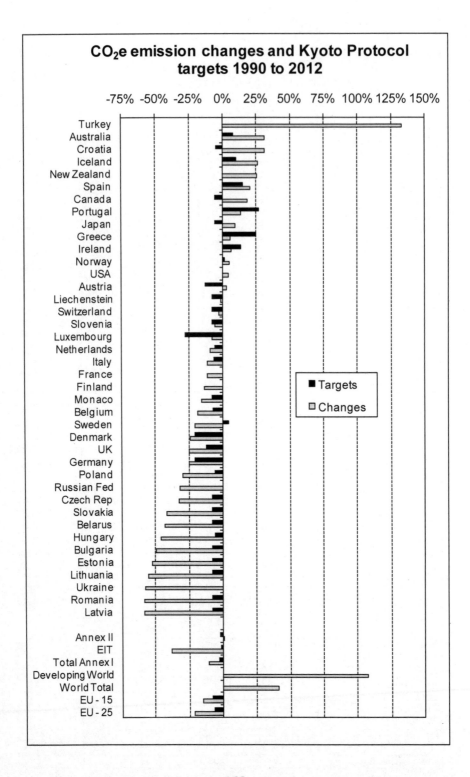

CO₂e emission changes and Kyoto Protocol targets 1990 to 2012

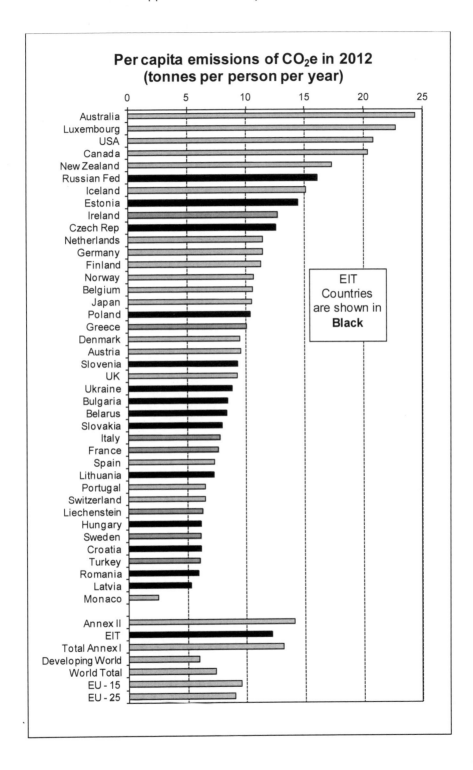

Per capita emissions of CO_2e in 2012
(tonnes per person per year)

EIT Countries are shown in **Black**

Appendix D

Sources Of Information

If this were intended as an academic book I would probably now add a list of references running into many pages. However, my primary intention has not been to prove particular points so much as to trigger your curiosity so that you will continue the search for yourself.

Some of the information presented is standard and well-known scientific background the validity of which is not in any doubt even though it may not be widely known among non-scientists. All the remaining information, including the statistics I have used as the basis for my own calculations, forecasts and predictions was obtained from sources on the Internet.

The text of the book usually provides enough information to enable you to search for the source yourself should you wish to do so. This has the advantage that in doing such a search in the future you may find more up to date figures than were available when I wrote a particular section.

I include only three specific sources of data as follows:

• Statistical information on production and consumption of fossil fuels and energy has been gathered together and published by BP. They provide extensive details on all types of fossil fuels as well as data on production of primary energy from hydroelectric, nuclear and other renewable sources. The information goes back in time and gives statistics for individual countries and for regions. The main source of the data used by BP is publications by the governments concerned. The data has been updated regularly on an annual basis and can be found online at www.bp.com/statisticalreview/.

• The second source of information is the Intergovernmental Panel on Climate Change (IPCC). A mass of information, which is continually being updated, can be found at www.ipcc.ch/. This has to be a starting point for any assessment of Climate Change.

• The third source of information is the database established by EIA, the US Energy Information Administration which can be found at www.eia.gov. This is government organisation which collates information from a wide variety of national and international sources. It was particularly useful when I was looking at recent trends in the production of renewables.

The Intergovernmental Panel on Climate Change was established in 1988 by two branches of the United Nations, the World Meteorological Organization (WMO) and the United Nations Environment Programme (UNEP). Three working groups were set up as part of IPCC. WG1 looks at the Science of Climate Change, WGII looks at Impact and Adaptation and WGIII looks at Mitigation. In the context of this book WGI is the most important as it looks at past trends in Climate Change, builds models and makes forecast for the future.

IPCC has recently been the subject of adverse publicity. Some of this arose from a report published by IPCC in 1990 which included charts suggesting the existence of a medieval warm period. This conclusion was changed in later reports without a clear explanation and there have been intercepted emails involving the University of East Anglia, which it was claimed, indicated that data had been fixed. As discussed in Chapter 6 there are other ways of interpreting both the data and the correspondence which do not suggest any dubious behaviour. Indeed a comprehensive analysis of data indicates that although there may have been a warm period in Western Europe in about 1200 this was not worldwide and the global average does not indicate any such warming.

In 2007 an IPCC report claimed that Himalayan glaciers would all have melted by 2035. In January 2010, a New Scientist article reported that this was an erroneous conclusion based on poor data. IPCC has subsequently accepted that this was a mistake and have apologised. This mistake has been used by the popular press and by sceptics to suggest that no information from IPCC can be trusted. This was certainly a mistake by IPCC but it does not mean that all their data is wrong.

The World's science academies created the InterAcademy Council (IAC) to get together the best scientists and engineers worldwide to provide high quality advice to international bodies, such as the United Nations and the World Bank on topics of global importance. IAC have recently produced a report on IPCC. Their overall conclusion was as follows:

"The process used by IPCC to produce its periodic assessment reports has been successful overall, but IPCC needs to fundamentally reform its management structure and strengthen its procedures to handle ever larger and increasingly complex climate assessments as well as the more intense public scrutiny coming from a World grappling with how best to respond to Climate Change. Operating under the public microscope the way IPCC does requires strong leadership, the continued and enthusiastic participation of distinguished scientists, an ability to adapt, and a commitment to openness if the value of these assessments to society is to be maintained"

In other words, IPCC is not perfect. But it can never be so as it is dealing with an increasingly complex situation in which there are considerable uncertainties. It usually attaches probabilities to its conclusions but these are often presented by the press as certainties.

The fact that it sometimes makes mistakes does not invalidate the majority of IPCC data and I have used it with confidence throughout this book.